QUOTIDIAN II

QUOTIDIAN II

Conveyed by Gudrun Cable

Portraits by Tracy Prescott

Sylvia Beach Hotel Drawings by Andrew Davies

RIMSKY PRESS
PORTLAND, OREGON

Library of Congress Catalog Card Number 89-062678
ISBN 0-9624011-0-2

Rimsky Press
707 Southeast Twelfth Avenue
Portland, Oregon 97214

For my parents,
Willard C. Johnson
and
Anne Michalov Johnson

PRELUDE

Everything that happened that night needed to happen. Somehow. I was alone in the library of the hotel. It was very late, probably close to 2:30 a.m. The hotel guests were all in their rooms, the lights were off, even the night clerk was asleep, bent over the registration desk with his head resting on a volume of *Moby Dick*.

I wished the man in Melville was still up. Or the couple from Virginia in the Alice Walker room. They had kept the dinner conversation lively with their tales of strange occurrences in their 200-year-old home. He wrote for a local newspaper and she led a book group. Both loved to talk books. The woman in Gertrude Stein had already stayed up late the night before. In fact, I think I wore her out by keeping her up way past her normal bedtime. She would argue politics and always brought with her a large collection of magazine articles to share.

No, tonight I was going to be alone. Don't get me wrong. I like being alone. I particularly like soaking in the hotel atmosphere at night. Listening to the surf, enjoying a one-log fire, drinking tea. This is the perfect opportunity to read a guest book from one of the rooms. Most of the comments made me feel so good about the hotel. Some would let us know how we could have done things differently, or how a particular room could be more authentic, but most expressed their delight in the place. Some would even thank me personally for the part I played in making the hotel happen. I would blush when I read those, even if it was in the middle of the night and no one was around.

Why did I want company tonight? I had given myself an assignment. I had to at least begin writing the introduction to *Quotidian II*. The quotes were collected, chosen, proofread, and the manuscript lay heavy on

my lap. It was time to present it to the reader. I felt the
same frustrations when faced with introducing the first
Quotidian eleven years ago. But then, however, I managed to travel to *The Haunted Bookshop*, a novel written by Christopher Morley, taking place in Brooklyn in
1919. In explaining my purpose to Morley's protago-
nist, Roger Mifflin, I inadvertently explained it to the
reader, bypassing the need for a formal introduction to
the book of quotes. That little sojourn in time had meant

The Sylvia Beach Hotel Library

a lot to me and I ached to go back. But I had no idea how it happened the first time and knew full well that we have little control of those matters.

I turned the dusty rose Queen Anne chair around in order to face the sea, leaned back and propped my feet on the window sill. It was momentarily clear outside. I counted the lights of eight or nine fishing boats and then the seconds between lighthouse beams. The panes of glass were fogged up around the edges as they always were at night. As I wiped the corners with a page of the morning's *Oregonian*, I saw a reflection of the fireplace and a couple of people sitting in the chairs on either side of it, both engrossed in reading. Once again, I counted the lights of the fishing boats and the moments between beams from the Yaquina Head Lighthouse, then I glanced back at the image of the library reflected in the window. I was in the company of two men, both apparently unaware of my presence.

As I stood up to rearrange the chair I felt the room spin, just a bit, as it frequently seems to during rough weather. I took a deep breath, sat down, this time with my feet tucked under me, trying to appear relaxed. I picked up a familiar book of William James' essays and eventually came to realize I was holding it upside down.

I glanced at the man sitting directly across from me. He was tall, with dark hair, eyes dark grey and set rather far apart. He didn't look particularly comfortable in what is rather a dainty wooden rocking chair. His knees stuck up and out and as I stared at their disproportionate length he suddenly slapped one of them so hard I almost fell over. What transpired then was ridiculous. He looked me straight in the eye with a long, serious, penetrating glare, then burst into laughter just as I burst into tears. The other man put down his book, grunted something at his knee-slapping companion, then brought me his handkerchief. Instead of going back to his chair he stood before the window in which I had first seen him. My fear subsided the instant I recognized him. It was R.L.S. in the flesh. Well, maybe not quite in the flesh.

"The Pacific. There's nothing like the Pacific," he sighed.

"I'm really sorry about all the stairs, I know they're hard for you," I apologized. "We couldn't afford an elevator. Believe me, it's amazing we ever opened at all."

"It's a fine hotel. And the climb doesn't bother me at all anymore."

"That's because he has a room named after him. I wouldn't complain if you had a room named after me!"

"Who ARE you?' I asked.

"Now I can see how most people would have no idea who I am. I came nowhere close to being famous. I was hardly published and died far too young. But I know that you've read every word I wrote and have carried my very thoughts into what's almost the end of the 20th century, I'd venture. Although this hotel doesn't seem a day beyond my time."

"You're Bruce Cummings," I whispered.

"W.N.P. Barbellion. If I wanted you to call me Bruce Cummings I would have signed my books that way."

"Listen, my friend, if I had read your books when you were alive, or if I had been alive when you were alive, or if I had been reading when you were writing, nothing could have kept me from beating a path to your doorway. I would have found you and I would have loved you. So I probably would have called you Bruce."

"It's such a dull name. But would you have loved me, really? Even after all my self-centered ramblings?"

"You were so alive in your diaries, even when you hated life and felt the injustice of your illness so acutely. You were so alive that now, 70 years later, you're more alive than many people who are physically alive today. You were terribly intent on defying time and space. Did it never occur to you that that's just what you were doing? By putting it all down on paper? I recall your once saying that you would have to be remembered for what you *could have done* instead of what you *did* because you were doomed to such an early death."

"No one ever thought I'd make it to 30, and I even ended my diary with my death two years before it really happened . . . just for a more dramatic ending!"

I shook my head. "No. I don't believe that's why. Your life and your death both had, or have, vague boundaries. Obviously."

Stevenson threw another log on the fire, then sprawled out on the braided rug in front of the fireplace, leaning on his right arm. His heavy boot almost knocked over the brass floor lamp next to my chair. It swung back into place as if not wanting to miss throwing light on any of our conversation.

"So what is it you're trying to do?" he asked.

I stared first at him, then his boot, then the lamp, then back to him. The only words that would come out were, "Who, me?"

"I was rummaging through *The Haunted Bookshop* the other day and Roger Mifflin told me you're finishing up another book of quotes. He also let on that you're quoting me this time in the new book, as well as in the original *Quotidian*. I'm rather curious about what I'm guilty of saying."

"Roger Mifflin does get around, doesn't he," I said.

"Listen, anyone who keeps books alive,—their characters, their stories, their authors—not only get around, but stay in motion, and remain inviting for all of us to pay our visits."

"I try to do that too, Mr. Stevenson, I really do."

"My dear, I know you do. But you're awfully busy staying up till all hours talking with the hotel guests. You know, the real ones. And thumbing through books looking for quotes and trying to put your own words down on paper. Sometimes you just don't pay attention to us."

"If it weren't for us," Barbellion interrupted, "human life would have a beginning and an end. It would be bordered . . ."

"And ordered . . ." I rhymed. "Thoughts risk losing their meaning unless they're put into action or to rest on a page in a book. But then they are lifted up and carried into a separate world each time a new reader sees them. Those words travel through time and space at the whim of each reader. It's a terribly exciting playground. . . ."

"And our emotions, our senses, and our reasoning are all invited to play," added Barbellion. "When we share a book, or read aloud, they become three-dimensional, dynamic beyond our singular imagination."

Barbellion came close to my chair and put a hand through my shoulder, through the back of the Queen Anne chair, and for all I know through the window and the ocean mist, and the darkness of night. "Goody, don't you see? I'm as alive as you'll let me be. I'm alive when you can presuppose my opinions, my feelings, my reactions. I'm alive as long as you can stretch my questions of 1918 into questions of today. Apply my theories, prove my guesswork, feel my pain, see my landscapes, hear my music!"

"You were a biologist. I know nothing of science. I carry you into my present day world because of what you wanted to know, not for what you knew. I'll champion the curious mind before all else."

"Why?"

"Because curiosity seems to be almost obsolete in our world. And disappearing right along with curiosity is dialogue."

R.L.S. cleared his throat, "Which is why, according to Roger Mifflin, you're publishing books of quotes, one for each day of the year written by one of us born on that day, and trying to get people to read the quotes then discuss them with one another."

"I'd use them for impetus to write in my diary," suggested Barbellion. "Even when I found it hard to talk with other people, it was always easy to talk with myself."

I smiled at my two very special guests. "In the meantime I get to know you all as I wander through libraries, centuries, cultures and countries, autobiographies, volumes of poetry, essays, letters and novels. I feast at your banquets of words and take tidbits back in little notebooks that end up being an assortment of statements, opinions, metaphors, and nice-sounding nonsense."

"How did the first book, *Quotidian*, turn out? Were you happy with it? Did it serve its purpose?"

"Yes, I think it did. At first I thought it had been an excuse to spend most of my time reading. But once the book ended up on the coffee tables in friends' houses, with pages dog-eared, and comments and family birth dates marked in the margins, I knew it was working. And I like the way different quotes have different meaning to each reader. When I ask friends to choose their favorite quote they seldom pick the same one. When asked which is my favorite, I've consistently answered: the W.N.P. Barbellion quote on September 7th." I pulled a copy of the book off the fireplace mantel and read aloud to my two guests:

> *Perhaps too great an enthusiasm exhausts the spirit. Love kills. I know it. The love of one's art or profession, passion for another's soul, for one's children, sap the life and blood and hurry us on to the grave ... lust of knowledge is as fatal as any other kind.*
>
> *I know it. But I don't care."*

"Will you promise to always use me on September 7th?" Barbellion asked me tenderly.

"And you on November 13th," I said to Stevenson, as I opened my new manuscript to the right page and handed it to him. "Here's what you're guilty of saying this time."

He glanced at the quote, then read with a sarcastic grin:

> *Some people swallow the universe like a pill; they travel on through the world like smiling images pushed from behind. For God's sake give me the young man who has brains enough to make a fool of himself!*

"Barbellion, my friend, you don't suppose I intended this for you now, did I?"

"Considering you died in 1894, when I was five years of age, you hardly had the opportunity to know what a fool I'd turn out to be!"

"Perhaps one person writes a truth and the next

falls into it, or evades it like the plague," answered R.L.S.

"It seems to me," I added, "that we have three worlds we can be sure of. The world that is real, the world that is in our mind, and the world that is in the minds of other people. There is something almost sacred about being let into this last world. Thank you both for writing down what you thought instead of just thinking it."

"As if we could restrain ourselves," Barbellion chuckled.

"You seem to be forgetting the composers, poets, and painters who put down on paper or canvas what they felt," added Stevenson.

But I hadn't forgotten. I visit with them often. There is an open door between my world and the world of the composers. It's never shut. But no point confusing the issue. Beethoven can go anywhere with me nowadays, thanks to cassette players, but I couldn't see trying to explain that to either of them.

A cheerful, young couple appeared from nowhere at the top of the stairs. I was about to introduce them as Zelda and Scott Fitzgerald but realized they were the Thompsons from Medford.

"Up already?" he asked me.

"Come join us for a walk on the beach!" she added.

It was first light, albeit a grey day. The air felt awfully damp. The fire had burned out. I was cold and tired. "No, you two go on while the tide's still out."

I put on a pot of coffee in the kitchen nook of the library then climbed the top flight of stairs to where we house the stacks of books. I built a nest of three or four beanbag chairs next to the window with the northern view. The Thompsons walked briskly down the stairs that led to the beach and were soon on the sand and then out of sight. I fell asleep.

Later that day I know I must have seemed preoccupied to the hotel guests and staff. Truthfully I felt empty and a bit agitated with myself. Moving among the three worlds seemed so natural, and yet so exhausting at times. The process of merging was almost precedented by the feeling of distancing myself.

I was overwhelmed by loneliness as I returned to the library later that afternoon. My manuscript was still on the floor in front of the fireplace. I picked it up, stuck it under my arm, put *Quotidian* back on the mantel. When I moved the dusty rose Queen Anne chair back to its corner, I found an old-fashioned white hanky on the floor. Holding it up to the window I could barely read the monogram "RLS." I threw it up in the air, then caught it and threw it up and caught it again. I rubbed one side of my face with it and then the other. A sure sign of madness, of course. But I hurried down the stairs skipping the last two, then rounded the corner by the registration desk in the lobby and pounded on the Robert Louis Stevenson door.

An elderly lady was occupying the room and was happy to greet one of the hotel proprietors at her door. She was arthritic and moved slowly over to the rocking chair in the corner. "How nice of you to visit with me," she said.

"Actually, I have a little item to add to your room." I lifted up the fern from the plant stand and laid out the hanky. "A perfect little table cloth, don't you think?"

We chatted a bit. I told her some of the history of the hotel and how different friends had chosen the authors and furnished the rooms to suit them. I must admit I was a bit more confused than I had been the day before. I wasn't sure whether my friend Linda chose Stevenson, or if he had chosen her. That man seemed to know what he was doing.

"I've got to get going," I finally told her. "I'm trying to write an introduction to *Quotidian II*, my new book of quotes." I still had the manuscript under my arm and held it out to her.

"Oh, may I read them?" she asked.

"Be my guest."

The Robert Louis Stevenson Room

QUOTIDIAN II

To behold the junipers shagged with ice,
The spruces rough in the distant glitter
Of the January sun
                                        Wallace Stevens

January 1

E.M. Forster
(b. 1879 - d. June 7, 1970)
English Novelist

I believe in aristocracy. . . . Not an aristocracy of power, based upon rank and influence, but an aristocracy of the sensitive, the considerate and the plucky. Its members are to be found in all nations and classes, and all through the ages, and there is a secret understanding between them when they meet. They represent the true human tradition, the one permanent victory of our queer race over cruelty and chaos. Thousands of them perish in obscurity, a few are great names. They are sensitive for others as well as for themselves, they are considerate without being fussy, their pluck is not swankiness but the power to endure, and they can take a joke.

                                        What I Believe

January 2

Isaac Asimov
(b. 1920 -   )
American Writer

To know all your neighbors on the global level does not mean that you will automatically love them all; it does not, in and of itself, introduce a reign of peace and brotherhood. But to be potentially in touch with everybody at least makes fighting more uncomfortable. It becomes easier to argue instead.

"The Fourth Revolution"

January 3

Douglas William Jerrold
(b. 1803 - d. June 8, 1857)
English Humorist

In this world, truth can wait; she's used to it.

"Punch," 1855

January 4

John Laursen
(b. 1946 -   )
American Book Designer

Capitalistic culture has a tremendous capacity to absorb efforts to mock it and then turn them into profit-making enterprises.

Personal Conversation

January 5

Umberto Eco
(b. 1932 -   )
Italian Writer and Editor

Perhaps the mission of those who love mankind is to make people laugh at the truth, *to make truth laugh*, because the only truth lies in learning to free ourselves from insane passion for the truth.

The Name of the Rose

January 6

Alan Watts
(b. 1915 - d. November 16, 1973)
American Philosopher

One of my missions in life, if I have any, is to show very rich and powerful people how to use their imaginations and enjoy themselves through being disabused of the notion that money and prestige have in themselves material reality. Love of money and imagination in spending it seem to be mutually exclusive.

In My Own Way

January 7

Zora Neale Hurston
(b. 1903 - d. January 28, 1960)
American Novelist

Ships at a distance have every man's wish on board. For some they come in with the tide. For others they sail forever on the horizon, never out of sight, never landing until the Watcher turns his eyes away in resignation, his dreams mocked to death by Time. That is the life of men. Now, women forget all those things they don't want to remember, and remember everything they don't want to forget. The dream is the truth. They act and do things accordingly.

Their Eyes Were Watching God

January 8

John Briggs
(b. 1945 -   )
American Writer

. . . the creator's task is very large. It is nothing less than the re-creation of the universe or, more precisely, finding or constructing a whole, integrated microcosm in order to reflect the whole macrocosm. To do this requires the creator's conviction that a microcosm of the whole can be made to reveal itself in some part: in a mathematical problem or field, in the story of a white whale, the harmonies of the tonic scale, the possibilities of primary colors, or the movements of the human body across a stage.

The Fire in the Crucible

January 9

Simone de Beauvoir
(b. 1908 - d. April 14, 1986)
French Writer

Words have this immense privilege: you can take them with you.

All Said and Done

Simone de Beauvoir

January 10

Lord Acton
(b. 1834 - d. June 19, 1902)
English Historian and Statesman

Power tends to corrupt, and absolute power corrupts absolutely. Great men are almost always bad men.

Letter to Bishop Creighton

January 11

William James
(b. 1842 - d. August 26, 1910)
American Philosopher

I merely point out to you that, as a matter of fact, certain persons do exist with an enormous capacity for friendship and for taking delight in other people's lives; and that such persons know more of truth than if their hearts were not so big.

Talks to Teachers on Psychology

January 12

Jack London
(b. 1876 - d. November 22, 1916)
American Novelist

The wolves have already begun to call me and it doesn't matter if they're still far away: as soon as they get close, I know I will follow them.

The Call of the Wild

January 13

George B. Leonard
(b. 1946 -   )
American Writer

When a great culture dies in a vacuum with nothing to take its place, chaos is almost sure to ensue. Today, there is a sense of a vacuum in that aspect of the present we call future, drawing us towards something we simply cannot conceive. The vacuum will be filled. If humor and intelligence and compassion are to have a hand in filling it, there is little time to waste. There is little time for the painstaking work of creating a new politics, a new education, a new culture that starts with what is best in the old—leaving off dominance and greed and narrow individualism but not respect for the personal nor appetite for exploration; following joy but not fearing pain.

The Transformation

January 14

Joseph Chilton Pearce
(b. 1926 -   )
American Educator and Writer

Spirit is the spine and skull of our developmental skeleton, and the spark of the intelligence behind it. Upon spirit all the various scientific ribs hang beautifully and make coordinated sense; without spirit we have fragmented nonsense.

The Magical Child Matures

January 15

Jean Molière
(b. 1622 - d. February 17, 1673)
French Dramatist

All men's misfortunes, and the appalling disasters of history, the blunders of statesmen and the errors of great generals, come from the inability to dance.

The Would-Be Gentleman

January 16

William Kennedy
(b. 1928 -   )
American Novelist

If you love something well enough, Grandmother Arch-
er told Helen when the weakness was upon her, you will
die for it; for when we love with all our might, our silly
little selves are already dead and we have no more fear
of dying. Would you die for your music? Helen asked.
And her grandmother said: I believe I already have.

Ironweed

January 17

William Stafford
(b. 1914 -   )
American Poet

Kids: they dance before they learn there is anything
that isn't music.

Stories that Could Be True

January 18

Kenneth Boulding
(b. 1910 -   )
American Economist

... we must not underestimate the fact that an agency like the Department of Defense has almost one lobbyist for every Congressman and has sold national greatness and militarism at least as effectively as Madison Avenue has sold detergents and deodorants. Between the two of them they could probably purify the hands even of Lady Macbeth.

"Economics as a Political Science"

January 19

Anton Chekhov
(b. 1860 - d. July 15, 1904)
Russian Writer

One has to respect even one's indifference, and not change it for anything, since indifference in a decent man is also a religion.

Diary Excerpt

January 20

Federico Fellini
(b. 1920 -   )
Italian Film Director

For a creative person to be criticized can be very dangerous. A creative person needs an atmosphere of ap-
proval. Like a fighter. You need to be drunk, you need
to be exalted, to believe in what you are doing.

Quoted by Hollis Alpert

January 21

Imre Madach
(b. 1823 - d. October 5, 1864)
Hungarian Poet and Dramatist

I doubt if I could forecast any future
that would be too auspicious for a parent.
Does not each new-born babe seem a Messiah,
A shining star to ev'ry family,
Though he may grow into the usual rascal?

The Tragedy of Man

January 22

August Strindberg
(b. 1849 - d. May 14, 1912)
Swedish Playwright

... it can be a duty not to say everything, not to see everything. That's known as tolerance—a thing we all need.

The Dance of Death

January 23

Hugh Prather
(b. 1938 -   )
American Writer

Fear is static that prevents me from hearing my intuition.

Notes to Myself

January 24

Edith Wharton
(b. 1862 - d. August 12, 1937)
American Novelist

To have as few numb tracts in one's consciousness as possible—that seems to me, so far, the most desirable thing in life, even though the Furies do dance in hobnailed shoes on the sensitive tracts at a rate that sometimes makes one wish for any form of anaesthesia.

Letter of April 30, 1909

January 25

Virginia Woolf
(b. 1882 - d. March 28, 1941)
English Writer

I can fasten on a beautiful day, as a bee fixes itself on a sunflower. It feeds me, rests me, satisfies me, as nothing else does.... This has a holiness. This will go on after I'm dead.

Diary Excerpt, 1932

Edith Wharton

January 26

Hans Selye
(b. 1907 - d. October 16, 1982)
Canadian Physician

My own code is based on the view that, to achieve peace of mind, and fulfillment through self expression, most men need a commitment to work in the service of some cause that they can respect. The highly motivated musician, painter, writer, scientist, businessman or athlete is terribly distressed if prevented from doing his or her work. For an active man or woman, one of the most difficult things to bear is enforced inactivity.

Stress Without Distress

January 27

Wolfgang Amadeus Mozart
(b. 1756 - d. December 5, 1791)
Austrian Composer

When I am, as it were, completely myself, entirely alone, and of good cheer . . . it is on such occasions that my ideas flow best and most abundantly. Whence and how they come I know not, nor can I force them. . . . Nor do I hear in my imagination the parts in sequence, but I hear them, as it were, all at once. What a delight that is I cannot tell.

Letter

January 28

Colette
(b. 1873 - d. August 3, 1954)
French Writer

Just imagine that I arrived home—intending to lunch alone—and I opened the drawer of my little desk to get some money—and a single letter fell out, a letter from my mother, written in pencil, one of her last, with unfinished words and an implicit sense of her departure . . . It's so curious: one can resist tears and "behave" very well in the hardest hours of grief. But then someone makes you a friendly sign behind a window—or one notices that a flower that was in bud only yesterday has suddenly blossomed, or a letter slips from a drawer—and everything collapses.

Letter of April 10, 1923

January 29

Romain Rolland
(b. 1866 - d. December 30, 1944)
French Writer

A hero is one who does what he can. The others don't.

Jean-Christophe

January 30

Barbara Tuchman
(b. 1912 - d. February 6, 1989)
American Historian

A phenomenon noticeable throughout history regardless of place or period is the pursuit by governments of policies contrary to their own interest. Why does intelligent mental process seem so often not to function? Why does American business insist on "growth" when it is demonstrably using up the three basics of life on our planet—land, water, and unpolluted air?

The March of Folly

January 31

Zane Grey
(b. 1875 - d. October 23, 1939)
American Western Novelist

Never insult seven men when all you're packin' is a six-gun.

Attributed to

Late February days; and now at least,
Might you have thought that
Winter's Woe was past;
So fair the sky was and so soft the air.

William Morris

February 1

Galway Kinnell
(b. 1927 -   )
American Poet

That is the way with poetry: when it is incomprehensible it seems profound, and when you understand it, it is only ridiculous.

Black Light

Gertrude Stein

February 2

James Stephens
(b. 1882 - d. December 26, 1950)
Irish Novelist

I believe that Nature is just as alive as we are, and that she is as much frightened of us as we are of her, and, mind you this, mankind has declared war against Nature and we will win.

The Crock of Gold

February 3

Gertrude Stein
(b. 1874 - d. July 27, 1946)
American Writer

One may really indeed say that that is the essence of genius, of being most intensely alive, that is being one who is at the same time talking and listening.

Portraits and Repetitions

February 4

Robert Coover
(b. 1932 -   )
American Author

... truth, when it is no longer pertinent, is not in the same sense truth any longer. ...

Gerald's Party

February 5

Adlai Stevenson
(b. 1900 - d. July 14, 1965)
American Statesman

With the supermarket as our temple and the singing commercial as our litany, are we likely to fire the world with an irresistible vision of America's exalted purposes and inspiring way of life?

New York Times, May 26, 1960

February 6

Louis Nizer
(b. 1902 -   )
American Lawyer

Not till the fire is dying do we look for any kinship with the stars.

Between You and Me

February 7

Hazel Hall
(b. 1886 - d. May 11, 1924)
American Poet

I am seeing so far tonight that I am blinded by the space between me and the inevitable.

Quoted by Susan Mach

February 8

Martin Buber
(b. 1878 - d. June 13, 1965)
Jewish Religious Philosopher

If you consider the individual by himself, then you see of man just as much as you see of the moon; only man with man provides a full image.

Between Man and Man

February 9

George Ade
(b. 1866 - d. May 16, 1944)
American Writer

Never accuse a man of being lazy. There is no such thing as laziness. If a man does not go about his work with enthusiasm, it means that he has not yet found the work he likes. Every mortal is a busy bee when he comes to the task that destiny has set aside for him.

"The Fable of the Old Fox and the Young Fox"

February 10

Bertolt Brecht
(b. 1898 - d. August 14, 1956)
German Playwright

We are traveling with tremendous speed toward a star
in the Milky Way. A great repose is visible on the face of
the earth. My heart's a little fast. Otherwise everything
is fine.

"The First Psalm"

February 11

Thomas Edison
(b. 1847 - d. October 18, 1931)
American Inventor

Everything comes to him who hustles while he waits.

Attributed to

February 12

R. F. Delderfield
(b. 1912 - d. June 24, 1972)
English Writer

Why should we spend any more of our lives than we need with a person like that, someone who finds pleasure in being miserable?

The Avenue Goes to War

February 13

Georges Simenon
(b. 1903 -   )
French Writer

History happens every day and the importance of events only becomes evident after the fact. One doesn't live with History, or rather one doesn't live History. One lives his little personal life, or that of a group, or of an instant of humanity, of an instant in the life of the world.

When I Was Old

February 14

Max Horkheimer
(b. 1895 - d. July 7, 1973)
German Social Theorist

If reason itself is instrumentalized, it takes on a kind of materiality and blindness, becomes a fetish, a magic entity that is accepted rather than intellectually experienced.

Eclipse of Reason

February 15

Alfred North Whitehead
(b. 1861 - d. December 30, 1947)
English Philosopher

It is the business of the future to be dangerous. . . . The major advances in civilization are processes that all but wreck the societies in which they occur.

Adventures in Ideas

February 16

Emery Reves
(b. 1904 - d. 1981)
Swiss Publisher and Author

It is a mysterious characteristic of human nature that
we are prepared to spend anything, to sacrifice everything, to give all we have and are when we wage war,
and that we are never prepared to take more than a
"first beginning," adopt more than "minimum meas-
ures" when we seek to organize peace. When will our
religions, our poets and our national leaders give up the
lie that death is more heroic than life?

The Anatomy of Peace

February 17

Robert Ornstein
(b. 1942 -   )
American Psychologist

Modern life impoverishes us when it comes to pleasure
and we've got to the point where people think it's bad
for their health. If something feels good or tastes good
or wastes time it's got to be hurting you. We'd be a lot
better off if we quit trying to micromanage our bodies
and started having more fun.

Interview with Michael Burgess

February 18

Toni Morrison
(b. 1931 -   )
American Writer

. . . to love anything that much was dangerous, especially if it was her children she had settled on to love. The best thing, he knew, was to love just a little bit; everything, just a little bit, so when they broke its back, or shoved it in a croaker sack, well, maybe you'd have a little love left over for the next one.

Beloved

February 19

Constantin Brancusi
(b. 1876 - d. March 16, 1957)
Romanian/French Sculptor

For art to become universal and free, one must be God to create it, a king to pay for it, and a slave to make it.

Aphorisms

February 20

Georges Bernanos
(b. 1888 - d. July 5, 1948)
French Novelist

. . . for if a man's flesh is weak, his nervous system is no less weak, and must yield, sooner or later, to the ever-increasing tension of a life whose normal activity is multiplied ten-fold, a hundred-fold, by the use of machines. The machine will give you leisure, so they tell idiots!

The Last Essays of Georges Bernanos

February 21

Anais Nin
(b. 1903 - d. January 14, 1977)
American Writer

Two people who love the dream above all else would soon vanish altogether. One of them must be on earth to hold the other down. And the pain of being held down by the earth, that is what our love for others will be.

"The All-Seeing"

Anais Nin

February 22

Arthur Schopenhauer
(b. 1788 - d. September 21, 1860)
German Philosopher

Every parting is a foretaste of death, and every reunion a foretaste of resurrection. That is why even people who were indifferent to one another rejoice so much when they meet again after twenty or thirty years.

Aphorisms

February 23

Karl Jaspers
(b. 1883 - d. February 26, 1969)
German Philosopher

The moment is the sole reality, it is reality in itself, in the life of the soul. The Moment that has been lived is the Last, the Warm-blooded, the Immediate, the Living, The Bodily-present, the Totality of the Real, the only Concrete thing. . . .

Psychology of World Views

February 24

Winslow Homer
(b. 1836 - d. September 29, 1910)
American Painter

The life that I have chosen gives me my full hours of enjoyment for the balance of my life. The Sun will not rise, or set, without my notice, and thanks.

1903

February 25

Meher Baba
(b. 1894 - d. January 31, 1969)
Indian Mystic

Love is essentially self-communicative. Those who do not have it catch it from those who have it. True love is unconquerable and irresistible; and it goes on gathering power and spreading itself, until eventually it transforms everyone whom it touches.

Quoted by Richard Alpert

February 26

Theodore Sturgeon
(b. 1918 - d. May 8, 1985)
American Science Fiction Writer

No planet, no universe, is greater to a man than his own ego, his own observing self.

"Thunder and Roses"

February 27

John Steinbeck
(b. 1902 - d. December 20, 1968)
American Novelist

Man might be described fairly adequately, if simply, as a two-legged paradox. He has never become accustomed to the tragic miracle of consciousness. Perhaps, as has been suggested, his species is not set, has not jelled, but is still in a state of becoming, bound by his physical memories to a past of struggle and survival, limited in his futures by the uneasiness of thought and consciousness.

The Sea of Cortez

February 28

Ben Hecht
(b. 1894 - d. April 18, 1964)
American Author

People are kindest to those they deceive. Thus good and evil balance.

Erik Dorn

February 29

Louis Fischer
(b. 1896 - d. January 15, 1970)
American Journalist

When the tongue preaches world government while the heart leaps to the military exploits and material successes of one's own nation, the tongue might as well be still. . . . Ultimately, no nation can enjoy successes that are not shared. There is no real peace or happiness while your neighbor down the street or ten thousand miles away is suffering.

The God that Failed

Ralph Ellison

A light exists in Spring
Not present in the year
at any other period
When March is scarcely here.

Emily Dickinson

March 1

Ralph Ellison
(b. 1914 -   )
American Author and Poet

Beware of those who speak of the spiral of history; they are preparing a boomerang. Keep a steel helmet handy.

Invisible Man

March 2

John Jay Chapman
(b. 1862 - d. November 4, 1933)
American Essayist and Poet

Knock and it shall be opened unto you: Seek and ye shall find: Ask and it shall be given unto you. This injunction goes to the very bottom of our functional life—contradiction, relaxation; work, rest. It is stated as religious truth with man asking and God giving; but it is a universal metaphysical truth, and one of the profoundest things ever said in psychology. You must have wished; you must have striven; you must have held on with intensity. But you must let go.

Letters and Religion

March 3

James Merrill
(b. 1926 -   )
American Poet

There are moments when speech is but a mouth pressed
Lightly and humbly against the angel's hand.

"A Dedication"

March 4

Frank Tannenbaum
(b. 1893 - d. June 1, 1969)
Austrian/American Writer

A formal ideology is an unconscious apology, a claim for validity that needs to be defended. A vigorous, spontaneous life calls for no explanation and overflows any doctrine.

"The American Tradition in Foreign Relations"

March 5

René Sully-Prudhomme
(b. 1839 - d. September 7, 1907)
French Poet

In my soul rages a battle without victor
Between faith without proof and reason without charm.

"La Justice"

March 6

Nikolai Berkyaev
(b. 1874 - d. March 23, 1948)
Russian Philosopher

The too perfect cease to create.

The Meaning of the Creative Act

March 7

Alessandro Manzoni
(b. 1785 - d. May 22, 1873)
Italian Novelist and Poet

For what, in the end, does history give us? Events that are known only, so to speak, from the outside, what men have done. But what they have thought, the feelings that have accompanied their decisions and their plans, their ... successes and misfortunes, the words by which they have asserted—or tried to assert—their passions and wills on those of others, by which they have expressed their anger, poured out their sadness, by which, in a word, they have revealed their individuality: all that, more or less, is passed over in silence by history: and all that is the domain of poetry.

On the Historical Novel

March 8

Gene Fowler
(b. 1890 - d. July 2, 1960
American Journalist

Writing is very easy; all you do is sit staring at a blank sheet of paper until the drops of blood form on your forehead.

Quoted in *Literary Almanac*

March 9

Mircea Eliade
(b. 1907 - d. April 22, 1986)
Romanian Mythologist

. . . the world . . . is not an inert thing without purpose or significance. For religious man, the cosmos "lives" and "speaks."

The Sacred and the Profane

March 10

Michel Eyquem de Montaigne
(b. 1533 - d. September 13, 1592)
French Writer

I speak truth not so much as I would, but as much as I dare, and I dare a little more as I grow older.

Essays of Montaigne, Book III

March 11

Douglas Adams
(b. 1952 -   )
British Novelist

The secret to flying is to throw yourself at the ground and miss.

Life, the Universe and Everything

March 12

Andrew Young
(b. 1932 -   )
American Politician and Minister

Nothing is illegal if 100 businessmen decide to do it, and that's true anywhere in the world.

Rolling Stone, March 1977

March 13

Janet Flanner
(b. 1892 - d. November 7, 1978)
American Journalist

Talent is a gift of the gods. It is the supreme good fortune in mysterious equipment. . . . Talent is inimitable, being genuine. It is thus the richest of all possessions.

Afterword: *The Cubical City*

March 14

Albert Einstein
(b. 1879 - d. April 18, 1955)
German/American Scientist

Everything is determined, the beginning as well as the end, by forces over which we have no control. It is determined for the insect, as well as for the star. Human beings, vegetables, or cosmic dust, we all dance to a mysterious tune, intoned in the distance by an invisible piper.

October, 1929

March 15

David Schoenbrun
(b. 1915 - d. May 23, 1988)
American Journalist

Perhaps some day man will achieve the kind of society where the individual's aspirations for life, liberty and the pursuit of happiness will not conflict with the needs of the community. Until then I will always have a soft spot in my heart for men who are not machines.

As France Goes

March 16

Anne Truitt
(b. 1921 -   )
American Artist

Of all the Ten Commandments, "Thou shalt not murder" always seemed to me the one I would have to worry least about, until I got old enough to see that there are many different kinds of death, not all of them physical. There are murders as subtle as a turned eye. Dante was inspired to instill Satan in ice, cold indifference being so common a form of evil.

Daybook

March 17

Karen Gordon
(b. 1944 -   )
American Writer

I wish people wouldn't say, "Excuse me," when I want them to step on my feet.

The Well-Tempered Sentence

March 18

Edgar Z. Friedenberg
(b. 1921 -   )
American Educator and Writer

We do indeed share a common culture and the common-
ness goes further. American mass gratifications, from
soft drinks to comic books and movies, have turned out
to be the common coin of mass culture the world over.
This is not conquest, but genuine cultural diffusion. All
over the world, man in the mass has turned out to be
exactly our type of fellow.

The Vanishing Adolescent

March 19

Philip Roth
(b. 1933 -   )
American Novelist

. . . The American writer in the middle of the 20th Century has his hands full in trying to understand, and then
describe, and then make credible much of the American
reality. It stupefies, it sickens, it infuriates, and finally it
is even a kind of embarrassment to one's own meager
imagination. The actuality is continually outdoing our
talents, and the culture tosses up figures almost daily
that are the envy of any novelist.

"Writing American Fiction"

March 20

Henrik Ibsen
(b. 1828 - d. May 23, 1906)
Norweigan Dramatist

Friends are dangerous, not so much for what they make us do as for what they keep us from doing.

Letters

March 21

Phyllis McGinley
(b. 1905 - d. February 22, 1978)
American Poet

We live in the century of the Appeal. . . . One applauds the industry of professional philanthropy. But it has its dangers. After a while the private heart begins to harden. We fling letters into the wastebaskets, are abrupt to telephone solicitations. Charity withers in the incessant gale.

"Aspects of Sanctity"

March 22

Louis L'Amour
(b. 1908 - d. June 10,1988)
American Western Writer

Much as I loved reading I was wary of it, for I soon saw
that much that passed for thinking was simply a good
memory, and many an educated man was merely repeating what he had learned, not what he had thought
out for himself.

Bendigo Shafter

March 23

Erich Fromm
(b. 1900 - d. March 18,1980)
American Psychiatrist

A genuine conversation is not a battle but an exchange.
The question of who is right and who is wrong is completely beside the point. It doesn't even matter whether
what the participants say is particularly cogent or profound. What matters is the genuineness of what they
say.

For the Love of Life

March 24

William Morris
(b. 1834 - d. October 3, 1896)
English Poet, Artist, Manufacturer

. . . if others can see it as I have seen it, then it may be called a vision rather than a dream.

News from Nowhere

March 25

Arturo Toscanini
(b. 1867 - d. January 16, 1957)
Italian Conductor

Mozart is so perfect that you are in the presence of something superhuman. All other music has faults— beautiful faults. They make it more human.

Quoted by Marcia Davenport

March 26

Joseph Campbell
(b. 1904 - d. November 1, 1987)
American Mythologist

. . . when you follow your bliss, and by bliss I mean the deep sense of being in it and doing what the push is out of your own existence, you follow that and doors will open where you would not have thought there were going to be doors. And where there wouldn't be doors for anybody else. There is something about the integrity of a life and the world moves in and helps.

The Hero's Journey

March 27

Budd Schulberg
(b. 1914 -   )
American Writer

Living with a conscience is like driving a car with the brakes on.

What Makes Sammy Run

March 28

Maxim Gorky
(b. 1868 - d. June 18, 1936)
Russian Writer

Everything that's best is always in a single moment.
How I long for different, more responsive, people—for
a different, less trivial, life, a life in which art would be a
necessity to all and at all times. How I long not to feel
myself unnecessary, superfluous.

"Enemies"

March 29

Sheldon Kopp
(b. 1929 -   )
American Psychologist

Escape is not a dirty word. None of us can face what's
happening head-on all of the time.

What Took You So Long?

March 30

Anthony Smith
(b. 1926 -   )
British Scientist

Every parent should also remember the existence of so-called backward learning, that undressing comes before dressing, emptying boxes is achieved long before they are ever filled, and a mess is made—repeatedly—before anything is tidied up. Much of learning proceeds from trial to error and only belatedly to success. We must first fall off our bicycles, and much of learning is achieved by being given the opportunity to fail.

The Mind

March 31

Octavio Paz
(b. 1914 -   )
Mexican Poet

Between never and always there lies in wait anxiety, with its thousand feet and its single eye.

The Monkey Grammarian

April comes like an idiot,
babbling and strewing flowers.

Edna St. Vincent Millay

April 1

Milan Kundera
(b. 1929 -   )
Czech/French Novelist

We can never know what to want, because, living only one life, we can neither compare it with our previous lives nor perfect it in our lives to come. We live everything as it comes, without warning, like an actor going on cold.

The Unbearable Lightness of Being

April 2

Émile Zola
(b. 1840 - d. September 29, 1902)
French Novelist

If you ask me what I have come to do in this world, I who am an artist, I will reply: "I am here to live aloud."

"Mes haines"

April 3

John Burroughs
(b. 1837 - d. March 29, 1921)
American Naturalist

We say that Nature is blind, but she has no need of eyes, she tries all courses: she has infinite time, infinite power, infinite space; and so far as our feeble minds can see, her delight is to play this game of blindman's bluff over and over to all eternity. Her creatures get life, and the joy and pain that life brings, but what is augmented, or depleted, or concluded, or satisfied, or fulfilled—who knows?

The Summit of the Years

April 4

Maya Angelou
(b. 1929 -   )
American Writer

Prejudice is a burden which confuses the past, threatens the future, and renders the present inaccessible.

"All God's Children Need Traveling Shoes"

Maya Angelou

April 5

William Fifield
(b. 1916 - d. December 14, 1987)
American Writer

It is not the breadth of perception of reality that sounds the clarion within us, but its humanity—the more a man is himself, the more he is us all. For the less he accommodates, the more he is human.

In Search of Genius

April 6

Lincoln Steffens
(b. 1866 - d. August 9, 1936)
American Journalist and Author

Heaven and hell are one place, and we all go there. To those who are prepared it is heaven. To those who are not fit, or ready, it is hell.

Autobiography

April 7

Gerald Brenan
(b. 1874 - d. January 16, 1987)
British Writer

We should live as if we were never going to die, for it is the deaths of our friends that hurt us, not our own.

Thoughts in a Dry Season

April 8

E. M. Cioran
(b. 1911 -   )
Romanian "Non-Professional Being"

What other people do we always feel we could do better. Unfortunately we do not have the same feeling about what we ourselves do.

The Trouble with Being Born

April 9

Tom Lehrer
(b. 1928 -   )
American Mathematician and Humorist

I know that there are people in this world who do not love their fellow human beings and I hate people like that!

"At the Drop of a Hat"

April 10

William Hazlitt
(b. 1778 - d. September 18, 1830)
English Writer

I think it is a rule that men in business should not be taught other things. Any one will be almost sure to make money who has no other idea in his head.

"Table Talk"

April 11

Ellen Goodman
(b. 1941 -   )
American Journalist

I read an article about birds that only feed their off-spring if they stay within the nesting circle. If one goes a foot beyond the invisible marker, the parents will ignore the cries of their own young.

Our society's a bit like that, I thought. We are for those who live within a certain circumference, or who capture our attention because they are extraordinary. We let some in and keep others out. And we don't ask ourselves often enough to expand the circle of caring.

Keeping in Touch

April 12

Frederick Franck
(b. 1909 -   )
Dutch/American Artist, Author, and Dentist

Looking and seeing both start with sense perception, but there the similarity ends. When I 'look' at the world and label its phenomena, I make immediate choices, instant appraisal—I like or dislike, I accept or reject what I look at, according to its usefulness to 'Me.'

The purpose of 'looking' is to survive, to cope, to manipulate . . . this we are trained to do from our first day. When, on the other hand, I SEE, suddenly I am all eyes, I forget this ME, am liberated from it and dive into the reality that confronts me.

The Zen of Seeing

April 13

Samuel Beckett
(b. 1906 -   )
Irish/French Playwright and Writer

Perhaps my best years are gone . . . but I wouldn't want them back. Not with the fire in me now.

Krapp's Last Tape

April 14

Anne Mansfield Sullivan
(b. 1866 - d. October 20, 1936)
American Teacher

Too often, I think, children are required to write before they have anything to say. Teach them to think and read and talk without self-repression, and they will write because they cannot help it.

Quoted by Helen Keller

Samuel Beckett

April 15

Henry James
(b. 1843 - d. February 28, 1916)
American Writer

We work in the dark—we do what we can—we give what we have. Our doubt is our passion and our passion is our task. The rest is the madness of art.

"The Middle Years"

April 16

Peter Ustinov
(b. 1921 -   )
British Actor

I do not believe that friends are necessarily the people you like best; they are merely the people who got there first.

Dear Me

April 17

Thornton Wilder
(b. 1897 - d. December 7, 1975)
American Writer

. . . the living too are dead and that we can only be said to be alive in those moments when our hearts are conscious of our treasure; for our hearts are not strong enough to live every moment.

The Woman of Andros

April 18

F. David Peat
(b. 1938 -   )
Canadian Physicist

Gravity is the neurosis of matter.

Lecture: June 30, 1989

April 19

Henri Poincaré
(b. 1854 - d. July 17, 1912)
French Mathematician

... it is by logic that we prove, but by intuition that we discover. To know how to criticize is good but to know how to create is better.

"Mathematical Creation"

April 20

Anne Murphy
(b. 1938 -   )
American Arts Lobbyist

You have to remember that we're in the thick of thin things.

Lecture: November 11, 1988

April 21

Josh Billings
(b. 1818 - d. October 14, 1885)
American Humorist

Don't marry a man to reform him; a man that can't reform himself is not worth reforming anyhow.

Uncle Sam's Uncle Josh

April 22

Vladimir Nabokov
(b. 1899 - d. July 2, 1977)
Russian/American Author

This, then, is IT: not the crude anguish of physical death, but the incomparable pangs of the mysterious mental maneuver needed to pass from one state of being to another.
     Easy, you know, does it, son.

Transparent Things

Vladimir Nabokov

April 23

J.P. Donleavy
(b. 1926 -   )
American/Irish Novelist

Please dear God stop us from being incurable. Just wrap us up in warmth and friendship. Make us more remembered than forgotten.

The Onion Eaters

April 24

Elizabeth Goudge
(b. 1900 - d. April 1, 1984)
English Educator, Artist, and Author

All we are asked to bear we can bear. That is a law of spiritual life. The only hindrance of the working of this law, as of all benign laws, is fear.

Green Dolphin Street

April 25

Walter de la Mare
(b. 1873 - d. April 27, 1956)
English Poet and Writer

. . . it is not when we are near people that we reach them
. . . but only by following their thoughts to where the
spirit within plays and has its being.

Memoirs of a Midget

April 26

Morris L. West
(b. 1916 -   )
Australian Novelist

It takes so much to be a full human being that there are
very few who have the enlightenment or the courage to
pay the price. . . . One has to abandon altogether the
search for security and reach out to the risk of living
with both arms. One has to embrace the world like a
lover. One has to accept pain as a condition of existence. One has to court doubt and darkness as the cost of
knowing. One needs a will stubborn in conflict, but apt
always to total acceptance of every consequence of living and dying.

The Shoes of the Fisherman

April 27

Edward Gibbon
(b. 1737 - d. January 16, 1794)
British Historian

I am indeed rich, since my income is superior to my expense, and my expense is equal to my wishes.

Memoirs

April 28

Robert Anderson
(b. 1917 -   )
American Playwright

Death ends a life, but it does not end a relationship, which struggles on in the survivor's mind toward some final resolution, some clear meaning, which it perhaps never finds.

I Never Sang for My Father

April 29

Edward Rowland Sill
(b. 1841 - d. February 27, 1887)
American Poet

The ill-timed truth we might have kept—
Who knows how sharp it pierced and stung?
The word we had not sense to say—
Who knows how grandly it had rung?

"The Fool's Prayer"

April 30

Annie Dillard
(b. 1945 -   )
American Writer

How can people think that artists seek a name? A name, like a face, is something you have when you're not alone. There is no such thing as an artist: there is only the world, lit or unlit as the light allows.

Holy the Firm

May 1

Pierre Teilhard de Chardin
(b. 1881 - d. April 10, 1955)
French Priest and Writer

To love Life so much, and to trust it so completely that we embrace it and throw ourselves into it, even in death —this is the only attitude that can calm and fortify you; to love extravagantly what is greater than oneself. Every union, especially with a greater power, involves a kind of death of the self. Death is acceptable only if it represents the physically necessary passage toward a union, the condition of a metamorphosis.

Quoted by Anne Lindbergh

May 2

Novalis
(b. 1772 - d. March 25, 1801)
German Poet

The sluggishness of our spirit oppresses us. But we can change our active life into fate. Everything seems to swamp us because we do not flow out. We are negative from choice. The more "positive" we become, the less "negative" the world, until there is no more negative. God wills gods.

Notebooks

May 3

May Sarton
(b. 1912 -   )
American Writer

Solitude exposes the nerve,
Raises up ghosts.
The past, never at rest, flows through it.

"Gestalt at Sixty"

May 4

Thomas Huxley
(b. 1825 - d. June 29, 1895)
English Writer

Every great advance in natural knowledge has involved the absolute rejection of authority.

Lay Sermons

May 5

Christopher Morley
(b. 1890 - d. March 28, 1957)
American Author

If you have no intellect, or only just enough to get along with, it does not much matter what you do. But if you really have a mind—by which is meant that rare and curious power of reason, of imagination and of emotion —it is better not to weary and wear it out over trifles.

Where the Blue Begins

May 6

Sigmund Freud
(b. 1856 - d. September 23, 1939)
Austrian Psychiatrist

A man should not try to eliminate his complexes but get into accord with them; they are legitimately what directs his conduct in the world.

Letter of November 17, 1911

May 7

Rabindranath Tagore
(b. 1861 - d. August 7, 1941)
Bengali Poet

The liberation of a tree is not the freedom from its roots.

Fireflies

May 8

Jane Roberts
(b. 1929 - d. September 5, 1984)
American Writer and Psychic

The atoms and molecules within you dream they are people. How real their dream is to you! How deep a trance is your life!

The Seth Tapes

May 9

Charles Simic
(b. 1938 -   )
American/Yugoslav Poet

The night fell quickly

Inside my empty bottle
I was constructing a lighthouse
while all the others
were making ships.

"Solving the Riddle"

May 10

Eric Berne
(b. 1910 -)
Canadian/American Psychiatrist

The aware person is alive because he knows how he feels, where he is and when he is. He knows that after he dies the trees will still be there, but he will not be there to look at them again, so he wants to see them with as much poignancy as possible.

Games People Play

May 11

Richard Feynman
(b. 1918 - d. February 15, 1988)
American Physicist

Our responsibility is to do what we can, learn what we can, improve the solutions, and pass them on. It is our responsibility to leave the people of the future a free hand. In the impetuous youth of humanity, we can make grave errors that can stunt our growth for a long time. This we will do if we say we have the answers now, so young and ignorant as we are. If we suppress all discussion, all criticism, proclaiming "This is the answer, my friends; man is saved!" We will doom humanity for a long time to the chains of authority, confined to the limits of our present imagination. It has been done so many times before.

What Do YOU Care What Other People Think?

May 12

Jiddu Krishnamurti
(b. 1895 - d. February 2, 1986)
Indian Lecturer and Religious Leader

A book can give you only what the author has to tell.
But the learning that comes through self-knowledge has
no limit, because to learn through your own self-knowledge is to know how to listen, how to observe, and
therefore you learn from everything: from music, from
what people say and the way they say it, from anger,
greed, ambition.

Think on These Things

May 13

Georges Braque
(b. 1882 - d. August 31, 1963)
French Sculptor, Painter, and Stage Designer

One cannot ask more of the artist than he can give, nor
of the critic more than he can see.

Diaries

May 14

Hal Borland
(b. 1900 - d. February 22, 1978)
American Journalist

When the legends die, the dreams end. When the dreams end, there is no more greatness. . . .

When the Legends Die

May 15

Katherine Anne Porter
(b. 1890 - d. September 19, 1980)
American Writer

One of the marks of a gift is to have the courage of it.

Writers at Work

May 16

Adrienne Rich
(b. 1929 -   )
American Writer and Poet

. . . the ultimate gift that love can offer—
The vital union of necessity
With all that we desire, all that we suffer.

"At a Bach Concert"

May 17

Erik Satie
(b. 1866 - d. July 1, 1925)
French Composer

Every morning with a medium soft brush, clean your
brain of all that it has eaten the previous day.

Quoted by Pierre-Daniel Templier

Erik Satie

May 18

Bertrand Russell
(b. 1872 - d. February 2, 1970)
British Philosopher

I call an impulse creative when its aim is to produce something which wouldn't otherwise be there and is not taken away from anybody else. I call it possessive when it consists in acquiring for yourself something which is already there, such as a loaf of bread. Now of course both have their function and man has to be sufficiently possessive to keep himself alive, but the really important impulses, when you're talking about the sphere of liberty, are the creative ones. If you write a poem you don't prevent another man from writing a poem. If you paint a picture you don't prevent another from painting a picture. Those things are creative and are not done at the expense of somebody else, and I think those things ought to have absolute liberty.

"The Role of the Individual"

May 19

Lorraine Hansberry
(b. 1930 - d. January 12, 1965)
American Playwright

Don't you see there isn't any real progress, Asagai, there is only one large circle that we march in, around and around, each of us with our own little picture—in front of us—our own little mirage that we think is the future.

A Raisin in the Sun

May 20

Honoré de Balzac
(b. 1799 - d. August 18, 1850)
French Novelist

From your bed to the frontiers of the universe there are but two steps: Will and Faith . . . Facts are nothing; they do not subsist; all that lives of us is the Idea.

Louis Lambert

May 21

Robert Creeley
(b. 1926 -   )
American Poet and Writer

. . . the bomb is human, rabbits didn't make it, or monkeys. It is a peculiar image, an actual artifact, of the human environment, and it's a very weird thing to have come up with, after all these years.

Contexts of Poetry

May 22

Peter Matthiessen
(b. 1927 -   )
American Author

All worldly pursuits have but one unavoidable end, which is sorrow: acquisitions end in dispersion; buildings, in destruction; meetings, in separation; births, in death. . . . Confronted by this uncouth specter of old age, disease and death, we are thrown back upon the present, on this moment, here, right now, for that is all there is. And surely this is the paradise of children, that they are at rest in the present, like frogs or rabbits.

The Snow Leopard

May 23

Margaret Fuller
(b. 1810 - d. July 14, 1850)
American Writer

The Woman in me kneels and weeps in tender rapture; the Man in me rushes forth, but only to be baffled. Yet the time will come, when, from the union of this tragic king and queen, shall be born a radiant sovereign self.

The Woman and the Myth

May 24

Bob Dylan
(b. 1941 -   )
American Songwriter

I hear the ancient footsteps like the motion of the sea
Sometimes I turn, there's someone there, other times
    it's only me.
I am hanging in the balance of the reality of man
Like every sparrow falling, like every grain of sand.

"Every Grain of Sand"

May 25

Theodore Roethke
(b. 1908 - d. August 1, 1963)
American Poet

What's madness but nobility of soul
At odds with circumstance?

"In a Dark Time"

May 26

Peggy Lee
(b. 1920 -   )
American Singer

I learned courage from Buddha, Jesus, Lincoln, Einstein, and Cary Grant.

Quoted by Joan Didion

May 27

Rachel Carson
(b. 1907 - d. April 14, 1964)
American Naturalist

If I had my influence with the good fairy who is supposed to preside over the christening of all children, I should ask that her gift to each child in the world be a sense of wonder so indestructible that it would last throughout life, as an unfailing antidote against the boredom and disenchantments of later years, the sterile preoccupation with things that are artificial, the alienation from the sources of our strength.

The Sense of Wonder

May 28

Warwick Deeping
(b. 1877 - d. April 20, 1950)
English Novelist

Man . . . is fighting a lone fight against a vast indifference. A gardener learns that. His flowers are fighting
the same sort of lone fight, and perhaps that is why he
loves them and pities them. Man invents religion to hide
the full horror of the universe's complete indifference,
for it is horrible. He tries spiritism. Oh,—anything to
escape, to colour the spectacles. I have always felt myself up against—not only the human scuffle—but
against the crushing—impersonal foot of the heedless
universal. It just treads on you, or it does not.

Sorrell and Son

May 29

G.K. Chesterton
(b. 1874 - d. June 14, 1936)
British Writer

The way to love anything is to realize that it might be
lost.

Tremendous Trifles

G. K. Chesterton

May 30

Randolph Bourne
(b. 1886 - d. December 22, 1918)
American Critic

I love people of quick, roving intelligence, who carry their learning lightly, and use it as weapons to fight with, as handles to grasp new ideas with, and as a fuel to warm them into a sympathy with all sorts and conditions of men.

Quoted by Sherman Paul

May 31

V. H. Flach
(b. 1929 -   )
American Metaphorist

There's only one FRUITFUL MOTIVE (all others Ulterior): like children, to love tuning-in to Universe structures and processes, and clarifying and integrating all one's own Individual Experience to and through some completed Forms—without interfering with anyone else doing the same.

"Toward Culture of Sojourns"

It is dry, hazy June weather. We are more of the earth, farther from heaven these days.

Thoreau

June 1

Henry Beston
(b. 1888 - d. April 15, 1968)
American Author

By day, space is one with the earth and with man—it is his sun that is shining, his clouds that are floating past; at night, space is his no more. When the great earth, abandoning the day, rolls up the deeps of the heavens and the universe, a new door opens for the human spirit, and there are few so clownish that some awareness of the mystery of being does not touch them as they gaze. For a moment of night we have a glimpse of ourselves and of our world islanded in its stream of stars—pilgrims of mortality, voyaging between horizons across eternal seas of space and time.

The Outermost House

June 2

Edwin Way Teale
(b. 1899 - d. October 18, 1980)
American Naturalist and Author

... better a single moment of awareness to enjoy the glory of the senses, a moment of knowing, of feeling, of living intensely, a moment to appreciate the sunshine and the dry smell of autumn and the dust-born clouds above—better a thousand times even a swiftly fading, ephemeral moment of life than the epoch-long unconsciousness of the stone.

"Autumn Across America"

June 3

Allen Ginsberg
(b. 1926 -   )
American Poet

America, how can I write a holy litany in your silly mood?

"America"

June 4

Harry Crosby
(b. 1898 - d. December 10, 1929)
American Poet

I believe in the Sun because the Sun is the only thing in life that does not disillusion.

Diary

June 5

Federico Garcia Lorca
(b. 1898 - d. August 19, 1936)
Spanish Poet and Dramatist

While a cathedral remains nailed to an epoch, giving a continuous expression of yesterday to the ever-moving landscape, a song suddenly jumps out of that yesterday into our present, lively and filled with beatings, like a late shrub, bringing the vivid light of old hours, thanks to the blast of the memory. . . .

"Children's Cradle Songs"

Thomas Mann

June 6

Thomas Mann
(b. 1875 - d. August 12, 1955)
German/American Writer

Between not willing a certain thing and not willing at all
—in other words, yielding to another person's will—
there may be too small a space for the idea of freedom to
squeeze into.

Mario and the Magician

June 7

Elizabeth Bowen
(b. 1899 - d. February 22, 1973)
English/Irish Writer

For you or me, to think may be to be angry, but remember; we can surmount the anger we feel. To find oneself
like a young tree inside a tomb is to discover the power
to crack the tomb and grow up to any height.

The House in Paris

June 8

Frank Lloyd Wright
(b. 1869 - d. April 9, 1959)
American Architect

Nature is all the body of God we mortals will ever see.

Quoted by Walter Sarrell

June 9

Raymond Fosdick
(b. 1883 - d. July 18, 1972)
American Writer and Lawyer

Organized government, organized business, yes, and organized religion level up our average but they also level down our best.

Chronicle of a Gentleman

June 10

Saul Bellow
(b. 1915 -   )
Canadian/American Writer

Your mother is the one goalkeeper you never can score with.

More Die of Heartbreak

June 11

Yasunari Kawabata
(b. 1899 - d. April 16, 1972)
Japanese Novelist

Any kind of inhumanity, given practice, becomes human.

House of Sleeping Beauties

June 12

Djuna Barnes
(b. 1892 - d. June 18, 1982)
American Artist and Writer

One must not look inward too much, while the inside is yet tender. I do not wish to frighten myself until I can stand it.

The Diary of a Dangerous Child

June 13

William Butler Yeats
(b. 1865 - d. January 18, 1939)
Irish Poet, Dramatist, and Critic

Man has wooed and won the world, and has fallen weary, and not I think, for a time, but with a weariness that will not end until the last autumn, when the stars shall be blown away like withered leaves. He grew weary when he said, "These things that I touch and see and hear are alone real. . . ."

"The Autumn of the Body"

William Butler Yeats

June 14

Vivian Gornick
(b. 1935 -   )
American Writer

I lived once in the American desert. The solitude opens up. It becomes an enormous surrounding comfort. But the solitude in the city is a confusing and painful thing.

In Search of Ali Mahmoud

June 15

Erik Erikson
(b. 1902 -   )
German/American Psychoanalyst

The true saints are those who transfer the state of householdership to the house of God, becoming father and mother, brother and sister, son and daughter, to all creation, rather than to their own issue.

Gandhi's Truth

June 16

Joyce Carol Oates
(b. 1938 -   )
American Writer

Society is caught in a convulsion, whether of growth or
of death, and ordinary people are destroyed. They do
not, however, understand that they are "destroyed."

The Profane Art; Essays and Reviews

June 17

Dean Ing
(b. 1931 -   )
American Writer

Failure for a man is like childbirth for a woman. If you
have your first one at middle age it can just about destroy you.

Wild Country

June 18

Gail Godwin
(b. 1937 -   )
American Writer

I was taught to believe that special patterns of words, or the resolutions of chords, or inspired slashes of colored pigment, on a flat surface, could make all the difference, between feeling you were an ordinary person, lonely, disappointed and trapped, and knowing you possessed a passkey to a kingdom with powers and privileges unlike any other.

A Southern Family

June 19

Elbert Hubbard
(b. 1859 - d. May 7, 1915)
American Author and Lecturer

Disgrace consists in mentally acknowledging disgrace.

"Philistines"

June 20

Lillian Hellman
(b. 1905 - d. June 30, 1984)
American Playwright

So at any given moment you're only the sum of your life up to then. There are no big moments you can reach unless you've a pile of smaller moments to stand on. That big hour of decision, the turning point in your life, the someday you've counted on when you'd suddenly wipe out your past mistakes, do the work you'd never done, think the way you'd never thought, have what you'd never had—it just doesn't come suddenly. You've trained yourself for it while you waited—or you've frittered yourself away.

The Autumn Garden

June 21

Mary McCarthy
(b. 1912 -   )
American Novelist

Learn to measure your capacities, never undertake more than you can do, then no one will know that you are a failure, you will not even know it yourself.

The Company She Keeps

June 22

H. Rider Haggard
(b. 1856 - d. May 14, 1925)
British Novelist

What is imagination? Perhaps it is a shadow of the intangible truth, perhaps it is the soul's thought!

She

June 23

John Solie
(b. 1937 -   )
American Artist

All men are not creative equally.

Personal Conversation

June 24

Norman Cousins
(b. 1915 -   )
American Journalist and Writer

If your ideas live in others, then you have indeed made a contribution to the immortality of the human spirit. If an idea lives in you that was born in others, you are benefiting from a grand continuity of the human spirit.

Saturday Review, 1956

June 25

George Orwell
(b. 1903 - d. January 21, 1950)
British Writer

. . . from the first articles to my latest book I have written so much, and perhaps too much, only because I cannot keep from being drawn toward everyday life, toward those, whoever they may be, who are humiliated and debased. They need to hope, and if all keep silent or if they are given a choice between two kinds of humiliation, they will be forever deprived of hope and we with them. It seems to me impossible to endure that idea, nor can he who cannot endure it lie down to sleep in his tower. Not through virtue, as you see, but through a sort of almost organic intolerance, which you feel or do not feel. Indeed, I see many who fail to feel it, but I cannot envy their sleep.

"The Artist and His Time"

June 26

Colin Wilson
(b. 1931 -   )
English Writer

We experience the ecstasy of freedom at the moment of becoming free—when the schoolboy escapes from school, when the grown man averts danger or emergency—just as you most enjoy the warmth of the bed when you have to get up in 5 minutes on a freezing winter morning. On a Sunday morning, when you can stay in bed, the warmth somehow loses its charm.

"Man is Born Free, and He is Everywhere in Chains"

June 27

Helen Keller
(b. 1880 - d. June 1, 1968)
American Author and Educator

I who am blind can give one hint to those who see: Use your eyes as if tomorrow you would be stricken blind. . . . Hear the music of voices, the song of a bird, the mighty strains of an orchestra, as if you would be stricken deaf tomorrow. Touch each object you want to touch as if tomorrow your tactile sense would fail. Smell the perfume of flowers, taste with relish each morsel, as if tomorrow you could never smell and taste again.

Quoted by Jack Smith

June 28

Luigi Pirandello
(b. 1867 - d. December 10, 1936)
Italian Playwright

Hang on to whatever you think true today, hang on to whatever you think true tomorrow, even if it's the opposite of what you thought true yesterday—or watch out!

The Emperor

June 29

Antoine de Saint-Exupéry
(b. 1900 - d. July 31, 1944)
French Aviator and Writer

I don't care if I'm killed in the war. But what will remain of what I have loved? By that I mean not just people but customs, certain indispensable intonations, a certain spiritual radiance. What will remain of the farmhouse lunch under the olive trees of Provence, or of Handel? The things that endure, damn it. What is valuable is a certain ordering of things. Civilization . . . has to do not with things but with the invisible ties that join one thing to another.

Wartime Writings; 1939-1944

June 30

Georges Duhamel
(b. 1884 - d. April 13, 1966)
French Writer

There are ancient graveyards which the centuries filled slowly, and where woman sleeps beside man, and the child beside the grandfather. But this burial-ground owes nothing to old age or sickness. It is the burial-ground of young, strong men. We may read their names on the hundreds of little crosses which repeat daily in speechless unison: "There must be something more precious than life, more necessary than life . . . since we are here."

New Book of Martyrs

A double row of huge old poplars beside the narrow brook swayed and danced in the gales, rustled in the late spring breeze, stood spirelike heavy in July sunlight.

Richard Aldington

July 1

Georg Christoph Lichtenberg
(b. 1742 - d. February 24, 1799)
German Aphorist

Probably no invention came more easily to man than inventing Heaven.

Aphorisms

July 2

Hermann Hesse
(b. 1877 - d. August 9, 1962)
German Novelist and Poet

And sometimes, when the black depths are silent, we can do even more. We can then be gods for moments, stretch out a commanding hand and create things which were not there before and which, when they are created, continue to live without us. Out of sounds, words, and other frail and worthless things we can construct playthings—songs and poems full of meaning, consolation, and goodness, more beautiful and enduring than the grim sport of fortune and destiny.

Gertrud

July 3

Franz Kafka
(b. 1883 - d. June 4, 1924)
Czech Writer

When you stand before me and look at me, what do you know of the pain within me, and what do I know of yours? And if I threw myself to the ground in front of you, and wept, and explained, what more would you know of me than you do of hell, when someone tells you it's hot and frightful? For that reason alone we human beings ought to confront one another as reverently, as thoughtfully and as lovingly as we'd confront the entrance to hell.

Quoted by Ronald Hayman

Franz Kafka

July 4

Neil Simon
(b. 1927 -   )
American Playwright

. . . people believe whatever they read. Something magical happens once its put down on paper. They figure no one would have gone to the trouble of writing it if it wasn't the truth.

Biloxi Blues

July 5

Jean Cocteau
(b. 1889 - d. October 11, 1963)
French Writer

Plans, marriages and journeys appear to me just as foolish as if someone falling out of a window were to hope to make friends with the occupants of the room before which he passes.

Opium

July 6

Gottfried Leibniz
(b. 1646 - d. November 14, 1716)
German Philosopher and Mathematician

The pleasure we obtain from music comes from counting, but counting unconsciously. Music is nothing but unconscious arithmetic.

Quoted by Oliver Sacks

July 7

Robert A. Heinlein
(b. 1907 - d. May 8, 1988)
American Science Fiction Writer

. . . I never do anything I don't want to. Nor does anyone, but in my case I know it. So please don't invent a debt that does not exist, or next you will be trying to feel gratitude—and that is the treacherous first step toward complete moral degradation. . . . 'Gratitude' is a euphemism for resentment.

Stranger in a Strange Land

July 8

Jean de La Fontaine
(b. 1621 - d. April 13, 1695)
French Poet

If a lute played itself, it would make me flee, though I like music extremely.

Psyche

July 9

Oliver Sacks
(b. 1933 -   )
British Physician and Writer

Each of us is a singular narrative, which is constructed, continually, unconsciously, by, through and in us— through our perceptions, our feelings, our thoughts, our actions; and, not least, our discourse, our spoken narrations. Biologically, physiologically, we are not so different from each other; historically, as narratives—we are each of us unique.

The Man Who Mistook His Wife for a Hat

July 10

James Abbott McNeill Whistler
(b. 1834 - d. July 17, 1903)
American Artist

... it took me two hours to do the painting but forty years to learn how to do it in two hours.

Attributed to

July 11

Max Jacob
(b. 1876 - d. March 5, 1944)
French Poet and Novelist

When you get to the point where you cheat for the sake of beauty, you're an artist.

Art Poetique

July 12

Henry David Thoreau
(b. 1817 - d. May 6, 1862)
American Writer and Philosopher

Pursue, keep up with, circle round and round
your life as a dog does his master's chaise.
                    Do what you love.
Know your own bone; gnaw at it,
bury it, unearth it, and gnaw it (still).

Letter of March 27, 1848

July 13

M.C. Richards
(b. 1916 -   )
American Teacher, Potter, and Poet

The child in man is his growing tip, alive throughout our
lifespan. . . . One of the labors of adulthood is to be-
friend in ourselves those handicapped and underdevel-
oped parts of our nature which we have set aside.

The Crossing Point

July 14

Northrop Frye
(b. 1912 -   )
Canadian Teacher, Author, and Editor

Thinking is not a natural process like eating, but an acquired skill like playing the piano: how well one will think at any given time will depend primarily on how much of it one has already done.

On Education

July 15

Iris Murdoch
(b. 1919 -   )
British Novelist

I hate solitude, but I'm afraid of intimacy. The substance of my life is a private conversation with myself which to turn into a dialogue would be equivalent to self-destruction. . . . I have never wanted a communion of souls. It's already hard enough to tell the truth to oneself.

Under the Net

July 16

William Irwin Thompson
(b. 1938 -   )
American Writer

Now we are taking another quantum leap in human culture. Marx would call it socialism; Boulding would call it post-civilization; and McLuhan would call it the electronic return to the tribe. The old art of the novel falls behind, for now reality itself becomes the work of art, and the lift-off of a rocket becomes a concert. And so the cycle spins around, as Vico, Marx, and McLuhan knew it would. In primitive communism, art was knowledge; in electronic socialism, it is knowledge itself that becomes the work of art. In a world in which men write thousands of books and one million scientific papers a year, the mythic *bricoleur* is the man who plays with all that information and hears a music inside the noise.

Passages About Earth

July 17

James Purdy
(b. 1923 -   )
American Writer

The theme of American culture, American commercial culture, that is, is that man can be adjusted, that loudness and numbers are reality, and that to be "in" is to exist.

Quoted in *Contemporary Novelists*

July 18

Shirley Solie
(b. 1940 -   )
American Friend

Your children, when grown, won't remember how clean the house was. But they will remember how you looked when you smiled and the sound of your laughter, long after you're gone.

Personal Conversation

July 19

Rosalyn Yalow
(b. 1921 -   )
American Medical Physicist

I think that the goals of women's societies should be to self-destruct. The most talented women should not be in women's groups but in men's groups. That's where the power is.

Time, May 1, 1978

July 20

Barron
(b. 1947 -   )
American Teacher

The planet desperately needs humans who know how to keep from repeating themselves and each other.

Letter of January 2, 1989

July 21

John Gardner
(b. 1933 - d. September 14, 1982)
American Novelist

True art clarifies life, establishes models of human action, casts nets toward the future, carefully judges our right and wrong directions, celebrates and mourns. It does not rant. It does not sneer or giggle. . . . It does not whimper or cower or throw up its hands and bat its lashes. It strikes like lightning, or *is* lightning, whichever.

On Moral Fiction

July 22

Edward Dahlberg
(b. 1900 - d. February 27, 1977)
American Writer

We are fatalists when we cease telling the truth, but, so long as we communicate the truth, we move ourselves, life, history, men. There is no other way. This is the simple epitome of the wisdom of nonresistance to evil. It is what Confucius, Thoreau, and Tolstoy taught. It is the incredible, the visionary way, and it announces treason and betrayal more boldly than firearms or airplanes.

"Thoreau vs. Contemporary America"

July 23

Raymond Chandler
(b. 1888 - d. March 26, 1959)
American Mystery Writer

There are two kinds of truth: the truth that lights the way and the truth that warms the heart. The first of these is science, and the second is art. Neither is independent of the other or more important than the other. Without art science would be as useless as a pair of high forceps in the hands of a plumber. Without science art would become a crude mess of folklore and emotional quackery. The truth of art keeps science from becoming inhuman, and the truth of science keeps art from becoming ridiculous.

Notebooks

Zelda Fitzgerald

July 24

Zelda Fitzgerald
(b. 1900 - d. March 10, 1948)
American Writer

It is a shock moving about as we do—or is it growing old—suddenly finding yourself in unremembered corners surrounded by a flood of forgotten associations.

Quoted by Nancy Mitford

July 25

Kip Courtland Smith
(b. 1966 - d. August 27, 1982)
American Poet

People are like clams
Hard on the outside
Soft inside.
Their shells are of various thicknesses.
Everybody is basically nice.
We learn to be cold.

"Hard Outside"

July 26

G.B. Shaw
(b. 1856 - d. November 2, 1950)
British Dramatist

This is the true joy in life, the being used for a purpose recognized by yourself as a mighty one; the being thoroughly worn out before you are thrown on the scrap heap; the being a force of Nature instead of a feverish selfish little clod of ailments and grievances complaining that the world will not devote itself to making you happy.

Introduction to *Man and Superman*

July 26

Carl Jung
(b. 1875 - d. June 6, 1961)
Swiss Psychologist

Nothing exerts a stronger psychic effect upon the human environment, and especially upon children, than the life which the parents have not lived.

The Spirit in Man, Art, and Literature

July 26

Aldous Huxley
(b. 1894 - d. November 22, 1963)
British Writer

There's something peculiarly base and ignoble and dis-
eased about the rich. Money breeds a kind of gangrened
insensitiveness. It's inevitable. Jesus understood. That
bit about the camel and the needle's eye is a mere state-
ment of fact. And remember that other bit about loving
your neighbours—the rich haven't got any neighbors.

Point Counter Point

July 26

Robert Graves
(b. 1895 - d. December 7, 1985)
British Poet and Writer

But friendship at first sight? This also
Catches fiercely at the surprised heart
So that the cheek blanches and then blushes.

"At First Sight"

July 26

André Maurois
(b. 1885 - d. November 24, 1976)
French Writer

In all circumstances we must defend our friends, not by denying evidence—for they are not saints and may have made mistakes, even serious ones—but by courageously affirming our fundamental respect. I know a woman who, whenever one of her intimates is attacked in her presence, merely states: "She is my friend," and refuses to say more. That, I believe, is true wisdom.

The Art of Living

July 27

Maurine Dallas Watkins
(b. 1896 - d. August 10, 1969)
American Poet and Writer

I've never in all my life erased a word—I tear up the pages and start over.

"Gesture"

July 28

Gerard Manley Hopkins
(b. 1844 - d. June 8, 1889)
English Jesuit Priest and Poet

What would the world be once bereft
Of wet and wildness? Let them be left,
O let them be left, wildness and wet;
Long live the weeds and the wilderness yet.

Inversnaid

July 29

William Dement
(b. 1928 -   )
American Sleep Researcher

Dreaming permits each and every one of us to be quietly
and safely insane every night of our lives.

Newsweek, November 30, 1959

July 30

William Gass
(b. 1924 -   )
American Writer

The artist's revolutionary activity is of a different kind. He is concerned with consciousness, and he makes his changes there. His inaction is only a blind, for his books and buildings go off under everything—not once but a thousand times. How often has Homer remade men's minds?

An uncorrupted consciousness . . . what a dangerous thing it is.

"The Artist and Society"

July 31

Jean Dubuffet
(b. 1901 - d. May 12, 1985)
French Artist

Ambiguous facts have always a great fascination for me, for they seem to me to be located at just those intersections where the real nature of things may be revealed.

"Landscaped Tables, Landscapes of
the Mind, Stones of Philosophy"

In August, the large masses of berries, which, when in flower, had attracted many wild bees, gradually assumed their bright velvety crimson hue, and by their weight again bent down and broke their tender limbs.

Thoreau

August 1

Herman Melville
(b. 1819 - d. September 28, 1891)
American Novelist

Oh, Time, Strength, Cash, and Patience!

Moby Dick

August 2

James Baldwin
(b. 1924 - d. December 1, 1987)
American Writer

I imagine that one of the reasons people cling to their hates so stubbornly is because they sense, once hate is gone, that they will be forced to deal with pain.

Notes of a Native Son

August 3

Marvin Bell
(b. 1931 -   )
American Poet

We all need a little more courage now and then. That's what I need. If you have some to share, I want to know you. Your criticisms you can keep to yourselves.

Quoted by Richard Kehl

August 4

Walter Pater
(b. 1839 - d. July 30, 1894)
English Essayist

To burn always with a hard gemlike flame, to maintain this ecstasy, is success in life.

The Renaissance

August 5

Wendell Berry
(b. 1934 -   )
American Writer

In representative government, the government is likely to represent the blindness of the governed.

The government, for instance, thinks that national defense is making weapons, and the people go along and pay for it. But soil conservation is elementary national defense. So is people conservation. So is the conservation of culture and intelligence. So is the conservation of political liberty and of the economic independence of households and communities. If the nation is to be defended, it may need many fewer warheads and many more real shareholders, people who own homes, homesteads, small businesses, small farms.

Interview in *Living Worlds*

August 6

François de Salignac Fénelon
(b. 1651 - d. January 7, 1715)
French Theologian

. . . youth is the only season in which human nature can be corrected, in youth the power of correction is without limit.

Telemachus Book XIII

August 7

Alice James
(b. 1848 - d. March 5, 1892)
American Diarist

The difficulty about all this dying is that you can't tell a fellow anything about it, so where does the fun come in?

Diary

August 8

Vauvenargues
(b. 1715 - d. 1747)
French Poet

More are taken in by hope than by cunning.

Reflections and Maxims

August 9

Philip Larkin
(b. 1922 -d. December 2, 1985)
English Poet

In everyone there sleeps
A sense of life lived according to love
To some it means the difference they could make
By loving others, but across most it sweeps
As all they might have been had they been loved.
That nothing cures.

"Faith Healing"

August 10

Witter Bynner
(b. 1881 - d. June 1, 1968)
American Writer

Words are hoops
Through which to leap upon meanings,
Which are horses' backs,
Bare, moving.

"Horses"

August 11

Louise Bogan
(b. 1897 - d. February 4, 1970)
American Poet

—O remember
In your narrowing dark hours
That more things move
Than blood in the heart.

"Night"

August 12

Edith Hamilton
(b. 1867 - d. May 31, 1963)
American Classicist

Pain is the most individualizing thing on earth. It is true that it is the great common bond as well, but that realization comes only when it is over. To suffer is to be alone; to watch another suffer is to know the barrier that shuts each of us away by himself. Only individuals can suffer.

The Greek Way

August 13

Bert Lahr
(b. 1895 - d. December 4, 1967)
American Actor

I think you laugh at a great comedian because you want to cry. Laughter is never too far from tears.

Quoted by John Lahr

August 14

John Galsworthy
(b. 1867 - d. January 31, 1933)
English Novelist

A philosopher when he has all that he wants is different from a philosopher when he has not.

The Forsyte Saga

August 15

Sir Walter Scott
(b. 1771 - d. September 21, 1832)
Scottish Poet and Novelist

Why is it that some scenes awaken thoughts which belong, as it were, to dreams of early and shadowy recollections? . . . How often do we find ourselves in society which we have never before met, and yet feel impressed with a mysterious and ill-defined consciousness that neither the scene nor the speakers nor the subject are entirely new; nay, feel as if we could anticipate that part of the conversation which has not yet taken place.

Guy Mannering

Sir Walter Scott

August 16

Charles Bukowski
(b. 1920 -   )
American Poet

Some people never go crazy, what truly horrible lives they must live.

Barfly

August 17

Charles Simmons
(b. 1924 -   )
American Writer

Near the end of his life he will be able to do whatever he wants with his time, civilization and nature having lost interest in him.

Wrinkles

August 18

Elsa Morante
(b. 1918 - d. November 25, 1985)
Italian Novelist

... of all the chasms through which we move blindly, none is so dark and so unknowable to ourselves as our own body.

Aracoeli

August 19

Gabrielle (Coco) Chanel
(b. 1883 - d. January 10, 1971)
French Fashion Designer

The most courageous act is still to think for yourself. Aloud.

McCalls, October 1967

August 20

Paul Tillich
(b. 1886 - d. October 22, 1965)
German/American Theologian

Love is the drive towards the unity of the separated.

Love, Power and Justice

August 21

Jean Rotrou
(b. 1609 - d. June 27, 1650)
French Dramatist

Friend who suffereth alone doth his friend offend.

Venceslas

August 22

Ray Bradbury
(b. 1920 -   )
American Science Fiction Writer

When faced with alternative courses and choices about my future I always ask my stomach, not my head, to decide. The head may rationalize . . . convince one to take a job that is really wrong, but the stomach knows, feels, smells sickness, if you are wise enough to pay attention to it.

"A Portrait of a Genius"

August 23

Will Cuppy
(b. 1884 - d. September 19, 1949)
American Journalist

All modern men are descended from wormlike creatures, but it shows more on some people.

Garden Rubbish and Other Country Bumps

Jean Rhys

August 24

Jean Rhys
(b. 1894 - d. May 14, 1979)
English Novelist

It is in myself.
What is?
All. Good, evil, love, hate, life, death, beauty, ugliness.
And in everyone?
I do not know everyone. I only know myself.
And others?
I do not know them. I see them as trees walking.

Smile Please

August 25

Kenneth Patton
(b. 1911 -   )
American Minister

Only a small minority of the people from any land have
sufficiently matured to become citizens of one world
and members of one humanity.

"A Letter to Japan"

August 26

Guillaume Apollinaire
(b. 1880 - d. November 10, 1918)
Italian/French Poet

... reality will never be discovered once and for all.
Truth will always be new.

"The Three Plastic Virtues"

August 27

William Least Heat Moon (William Trogdon)
(b. 1939 -   )
American Author

The wanderer's danger is to find comfort.

Blue Highways

August 28

Johann Wolfgang von Goethe
(b. 1749 - d. March 22, 1832)
German Poet

We may imagine ourselves in any situation we like, but we always think of ourselves as seeing—I believe that the reason man dreams is because he should not stop seeing. Some day perhaps the inner light will shine forth from us, and then we shall need no other light.

Elective Affinities

August 29

Charles Kettering
(b. 1876 - d. November 26, 1958)
American Inventor

We should all be concerned about the future because we will have to spend the rest of our lives there.

Seed for Thought

August 30

John Gunther
(b. 1901 - d. May 29, 1970)
American Journalist and Author

Ours is the only country deliberately founded on a good idea.

Inside USA

August 31

Théophile Gautier
(b. 1811 - d. October 23, 1872)
French Dramatist and Essayist

When an object becomes useful it ceases to be beautiful.

"L'Art"

September twenty-second, Sir, the bough cracks with the unpicked apples, and at dawn the small-mouth bass breaks water, gorged with spawn.

Robert Lowell

September 1

Blaise Cendrars
(b. 1887 - d. January 22, 1961)
French Writer

Only a soul full of despair can ever attain serenity and, to be in despair, you must have loved a good deal and still love the world.

A Night in the Forest

September 2

Miguel de Unamuno y Jugo
(b. 1864 - d. December 31, 1936)
Spanish Philosopher

There are people who appear to think only with the brain, or with whatever may be the specific thinking organ; while others with all the body and all the soul, with the blood, with the marrow of the bones, with the heart, with the lungs, with the belly, with the life.

The Tragic Sense of Life

September 3

Loren Eiseley
(b. 1907 - d. July 9, 1977)
American Anthropologist and Naturalist

We forget that nature itself is one vast miracle transcending the reality of night and nothingness. We forget that each one of us in his personal life repeats that miracle.

The Firmament of Time

Loren Eiseley

September 4

Ivan Illich
(b. 1926 -   )
Austrian/American Educational Theorist

As people become apt pupils in learning how to need, the ability to shape wants from experienced satisfaction becomes a rare competence of the very rich or the seriously undersupplied.

Toward a History of Needs

September 5

Arthur Koestler
(b. 1905 - d. March 3, 1983)
Hungarian/English Novelist and Essayist

. . . Einstein's space is no closer to reality than Van Gogh's sky. The glory of science is not in a truth more absolute than the truth of Bach or Tolstoy, but in the act of creation itself. The scientist's discoveries impose his own order on chaos, as the composer or painter imposes his; an order that always refers to limited aspects of reality, and is based on the observer's frame of reference, which differs from period to period as a Rembrandt nude differs from a nude by Manet.

The Act of Creation

September 6

Robert Pirsig
(b. 1928 -   )
American Writer

Laws of nature are human inventions, like ghosts. Laws of logic, of mathematics are also human inventions, like ghosts. The whole blessed thing is a human invention, including the idea that it isn't a human invention.

The world has no existence whatsoever outside the human imagination. It's all a ghost, and in antiquity was so recognized as a ghost, the whole blessed world we live in. It's run by ghosts. We see what we see because these ghosts show it to us, ghosts of Moses and Christ and the Buddha, and Plato, and Descartes, and Rousseau and Jefferson and Lincoln, on and on. Isaac Newton is a very good ghost. One of the best. Your common sense is nothing more than the voices of thousands and thousands of these ghosts from the past. Ghosts and more ghosts. Ghosts trying to find their place among the living.

Zen and the Art of Motorcycle Maintenance

September 7

W.N.P. Barbellion
(b. 1889 - d. October 22, 1919)
English Diarist and Biologist

Life pursues me like a fury. Everything, at all times, I am feeling, thinking, hoping, hating, loving, cheering. It is impossible to escape.

Enjoying Life

September 8

Siegfried Sassoon
(b. 1886 - d. September 1, 1967)
English Author

How good it is to get the savour of time past; what living skies, what crowds of faces, what unending murmur of voices, mingle with the sounds and visions of to-day; for to-day is always the event; all the yesterdays are windows looking out on unbounded serenity, and dreams written on the darkness; and suspended actions refashion themselves in silence, playing the parts they learned, at a single stroke of thought.

Diaries: 1915-1918

September 9

Paul Goodman
(b. 1911 - d. August 2, 1972)
American Writer

The American faces that used to be so beautiful, so resolute, and yet poignantly open and innocent, are looking ugly these days, hard, thin-lipped, and like innocence spoilt without having become experienced. For our sake, as well as your own, be wary of us.

The Moral Ambiguity of America

September 10

Franz Werfel
(b. 1890 - d. August 26, 1945)
Czech/German Writer

There is nothing more wonderful in the midst of a hard and strenuous life than to awaken with the feeling that morning has come and to find that it is still the middle of the night and that there is still an eternity of sleep ahead.

Star of the Unborn

September 11

D. H. Lawrence
(b. 1885 - d. March 2, 1930)
English Novelist and Poet

Things men have made with wakened hands, and put soft life into are awake through years with transferred touch, and go on glowing for long years.

And for this reason, some old things are lovely, warm still with the life of forgotten men who made them.

"Pansies"

September 12

H. L. Mencken
(b. 1880 - d. January 29, 1956)
American Editor and Essayist

Democracy is the theory that the average man knows what he wants and deserves to get it GOOD AND HARD.

"Definition of Puritanism"

September 13

J. B. Priestley
(b. 1894 - d. August 14, 1984)
English Writer

Sooner or later, some of us will have to buy an instrument that can switch on silence instead of sound.

"Another Revolution"

September 14

Sydney Harris
(b. 1917 - d. December 7, 1986)
American Journalist

Nobody knows himself until he has come face to face
with calamity; it is only in crises that we learn our true
identity; and many a man has gone through life thinking
he was strong, when he was only safe.

Last Things First

September 15

La Rochefoucauld
(b. 1613 - d. March 17, 1680)
French Writer

How is it that our memory is good enough to remember
the slightest triviality in our lives, but not good enough to
remember how often we have told it to the same person.

Maxims

September 16

Lawrence J. Peters
(b. 1919 -   )
American Writer

Don't expect much of a country in which half the people
are below average.

Peter's Quotations

September 17

Mary Stewart
(b. 1916 -   )
English Novelist

It is hard to tell, when the gods trail the shadows of
foreknowledge across the light, whether the cloud is
one that will blot out a king's realm, or make a child cry
in its sleep.

The Crystal Cave

September 18

Greta Garbo
(b. 1906 -   )
Swedish Actress

I sometimes feel that I have sacrificed my real self to become an image: the image of a beautiful woman who can gratify each of thousands of hopeless expectations and frustrated desires. The real Greta Garbo has been transformed into the vision of what the adolescent will never find, what the middle-aged man has spent fifty futile years searching for, what this woman or that wishes desperately she were so that she could hold on to the man who is slipping away from her. . . . I hide out of pity for all these people, for all of them, because I don't want them to know that I do not really exist.

Interview

September 19

Rachel L. Field
(b. 1894 - d. March 15, 1942)
American Writer

. . . I am not the first, and I shall not be the last, to try to make a bowstring into an anchor chain.

And Now Tomorrow

September 20

Max Perkins
(b. 1884 - d. June 17, 1947)
American Editor

The most important obligation of friendship is to listen.

Quoted by Steven Berg

September 21

Richard Kehl
(b. 1936 -   )
American Artist

Quite literally, a man's memory is what he forgets with.

Personal Notes

September 22

Lord Chesterfield
(b. 1694 - d. March 24, 1773)
English Courtier, Orator, and Wit

Whoever is in a hurry shows that the thing he is about is
too big for him.

Letter of August 10, 1749

September 23

Louise Nevelson
(b. 1900 - d. April 17, 1988)
Russian/American Sculptress

What I seek is anything that will work for me. I'll use a
lie if it works, and that's the truth. Look at this skirt I'm
wearing. This whole outfit is being held up by a safety
pin. That pin is a lie, the missing button is the truth, but
the lie works for me.

Quoted by Arnold B. Glimcher

Florida Scott-Maxwell

September 24

Florida Scott-Maxwell
(b. 1884 - d. 1979)
American Writer

I wonder why love is so often equated with joy when it is everything else as well. Devastation, balm, obsession, granting and receiving excessive value, and losing it again. It is recognition, often of what you are not but might be.

Measure of My Day

September 25

Glenn Gould
(b. 1932 - d. October 4, 1982)
Canadian Pianist and Composer

It's true that I've driven through a number of red lights. But on the other hand, I've stopped at a lot of green ones I've never gotten credit for.

Quoted by Alfred Bester

September 26

T. S. Eliot
(b. 1888 - d. January 4, 1965)
American-born British Poet

Do I dare
Disturb the universe?
In a minute there is time
For decisions and revisions which a minute will reverse.

"Love Song of J. Alfred Prufrock"

September 27

Jack Goldstein
(b. 1945 -   )
American Artist

The by-products of culture symbolize our position in the world. The details of living prevent us from seeing symbolically.

"Mind Over Matter"

September 28

Hugh Mearns
(b. 1875 - d. March 13, 1965)
American Professor

Keep good natured . . . no matter what you find . . . you did not invent life, so do not hold yourself responsible for what life does to you; decline to lay blame upon anyone.

The Creative Adult

September 29

Elizabeth Gaskell
(b. 1810 - d. November 12, 1865)
English Novelist

I'll not listen to reason. . . . Reason always means what someone else has to say.

Cranford

September 30

W.S. Merwin
(b. 1927 -   )
American Poet

To succeed consider what is as though it were past
Deem yourself inevitable and take credit for it
If you find you no longer believe enlarge the temple.

"A Scale in Man"

October 1

Daniel Boorstin
(b. 1914 -   )
American Historian

We might say now that chewing gum is the television of
the mouth. There is no danger so long as we do not think
that by chewing gum we are getting nourishment. But
the Graphic Revolution has offered us the means of
making all experience a form of mental chewing gum,
which can be continually sweetened to give us the illu-
sion that we are being nourished.

The Image or What Happened to the American Dream

October 2

Wallace Stevens
(b. 1879 - d. August 22, 1955)
American Poet

God is gracious to some very peculiar people.

Letters

October 3

Gore Vidal
(b. 1925 -   )
American Playwright, Novelist, and Critic

Stendhal wrote that politics in a work of art is like a pistol shot at a concert. But that was another century. Today the pistol shots are the concert while the work of art is the discordant interruption.

Reflections upon a Sinking Ship

Gore Vidal

October 4

Christopher Alexander
(b. 1936 -   )
American Architect and Educator

When you build a thing you cannot merely build that thing in isolation, but must also repair the world around it, and within it, so that the larger world at that one place becomes more coherent, and more whole; and the thing which you make takes its place in the web of nature, as you make it.

A Pattern Language

October 5

Philip Berrigan
(b. 1923 -   )
American Clergyman

When peacemakers fear dishonesty in their rhetoric more than they fear consequences, their fears will have become human, inspiring a clarity of passion and a style of genuine service.

A Punishment for Peace

October 6

George Horace Lorimer
(b. 1867 - d. November 22, 1937)
American Editor

Learn a man's limitations. If you make him bite off more than he can chew, don't get mad at him if he has to spit it out.

Letters to His Son

October 7

R.D. Laing
(b. 1927 -   )
American Psychiatrist

We live in a moment of history where change is so speeded up that we begin to see the present only when it is already disappearing.

The Politics of Experience

October 8

Frank Herbert
(b. 1920 - d. February 11, 1986)
American Author

Fear is the mind-killer. Fear is the little death that brings total obliteration. I will face my fear. I will permit it to pass over me and through me. And when it has gone past me I will turn to see fear's path. Where the fear has gone there will be nothing. Only I will remain.

Dune

October 9

Esther Froistad
(b. 1901 -   )
American Writer

I'll take my epiphany
every day, without fanfare;
The gold of the sun anytime . . .
Sunrise, sunset, whenever.
Or rain glazing dull colors
into exaggerated brightness
Freshness of unpolluted
early morning . . .

Epiphany

October 10

John Hollander
(b. 1929 -   )
American Poet

Doing and then having done is having ruled and
    commanded
A world, a self, a poem, a heartbeat in the moonlight.

The Quest of the Gole

October 11

François Mauriac
(b. 1885 - d. September 1, 1970)
French Novelist and Playwright

One must hope to grow old keeping one's life and back-
ground richly filled, hope to live so that people need us
and we need them until the end.

Second Thoughts

October 12

Eugenio Montale
(b. 1896 - d. September 12, 1981)
Italian Poet and Writer

The man of today has inherited a nervous system which cannot withstand the present conditions of life. While waiting for the man of tomorrow to be born, the man of today reacts to the altered conditions not by standing up to them or by endeavoring to resist their blows, but by turning into a mass.

Poet in Our Time

October 13

Herbert Block
(b. 1909 -   )
American Cartoonist

We need to stop letting our values be marked down, taking whatever we can get "as is," with service that's not as was, and at prices that never were.

Herblock on All Points

October 14

E.E. Cummings
(b. 1894 - d. September 3, 1962)
American Poet

... it's you—nobody else—who determine your destiny and decide your fate. Nobody else can be alive for you; nor can you be alive for anybody else. Toms can be Dicks and Dicks can be Harrys, but none of them can ever be you. There's the artist's responsibility; and the most awful responsibility on earth. If you can take it, take it—and be. If you can't, cheer up and go about other people's business; and do (or undo) till you drop.

"Nonlecture 2"

October 15

C.P. Snow
(b. 1905 -   )
English Novelist and Scientist

Without thinking about it they respond alike. That is what a culture means.

"Two Cultures and the Scientific Revolution"

October 16

Eugene O'Neill
(b. 1888 - d. November 27, 1953)
American Playwright

Pity the man who loves what death can touch.

Mourning Becomes Electra

October 17

Nathanael West
(b. 1903 - d. December 22, 1940)
American Novelist

Men have always fought their misery with dreams. Although dreams were once powerful, they have been made puerile by the movies, radio and newspapers. Among many betrayals this one is the worst.

Miss Lonelyhearts

October 18

Shunryu Suzuki
(b. 1870 - d. July 12, 1966)
Japanese Educator and Philosopher

That's why I love philosophy: no one wins.

Quoted by John Cage

October 19

John le Carré
(b. 1931 -   )
British Novelist

That's how we spend our lives, isn't it? Looking for people we'll never find.

A Small Town in Germany

October 20

John Dewey
(b. 1859 - d. June 1, 1952)
American Philosopher and Educator

Conformity is a name for the absence of vital inter-play:
the arrest and benumbing of communication.

Individualism Old and New

October 21

Ursula LeGuin
(b. 1929 -   )
American Writer

But old women are different from everybody else, they
say what they think.

The Word for World Is Forest

October 22

Doris Lessing
(b. 1919 -   )
British Novelist

Like the jaded woman of our dead civilization, she knew love like a fever, to be suffered, to be lived through: "falling in love" was an illness to be endured, a trap which might lead her to betray her own nature, her good sense, and her real purposes. It was not a door to anything but itself: not a key to living. It was a state, a condition, sufficient unto itself: almost independent of its object . . . "being in love."

The Memoirs of a Survivor

October 23

Nick Tosches
(b. 1949 -   )
American Author

There was more mystery, more power, in Elvis, singer of "Danny Boy," than in Bob Dylan, utterer of hermetic ironies. It is the sheer, superhuman tastelessness of Elvis that shakes the mind. In 1965, as Western Civilization lay on its tummy peeking over the brink at the rapids of psilocybin and "I Can't Get No Satisfaction," Elvis, for all the world to see, was hopping about singing "Do the Clam."

Country

Doris Lessing

October 24

Brenda Ueland
(b. 1891 - d. March 5, 1985)
American Writer and Educator

If it is true to you, it is true. Another truth may take its place later. What comes truly from me is true, whether anybody believes it or not. It is MY truth.

Therefore, when you write, speak with complete self trust and do not timidly qualify and feel the ice of well authenticated literary usage and critical soundness —so afraid when you have finished writing that they will riddle you with holes. Let them. Later if you find what you wrote isn't true, accept the new truth. Consistency is the horror of the world.

If You Want to Write

October 25

Anne Tyler
(b. 1941 -   )
American Novelist

You're given years and years of lessons in how to balance equations, which Lord knows you will never have to do in normal life. But how about parenthood? Or marriage, either, come to think of it. Before you can drive a car you need a state-approved course of instruction, but driving a car is nothing, nothing, compared to living day in and day out with a husband and raising up a new human being.

Breathing Lessons

October 26

Domenico Scarlatti
(b. 1685 - d. July 23, 1757)
Italian Composer

Show yourself more human than critical and your pleasure will increase.

Quoted by John K. Williams

October 27

Fran Lebowitz
(b. 1951 -   )
American Writer

I believe that all people should have warm clothing, sufficient food and adequate shelter. I do feel, however, that unless they are willing to behave in an acceptable manner they should bundle up, chow down, and stay home.

Metropolitan Life

October 28

Evelyn Waugh
(b. 1903 - d. April 10, 1966)
English Novelist

It's the secret of social ease in this country. They talk entirely for their own pleasure. Nothing they say is designed to be heard.

The Loved One

October 29

Jean Giraudoux
(b. 1882 - d. January 31, 1944)
French Playwright

One has to fear everything—or nothing.

Amphitryon 38

October 30

Paul Valéry
b. 1871 - d. July 20, 1945)
French Poet and Critic

... disorder is the condition of the mind's fertility: it contains the mind's promise. ...

"The Course in Poetics: First Lesson"

October 31

John Keats
(b. 1795 - d. February 23, 1821)
English Poet

I feel more and more every day, as my imagination strengthens, that I do not live in this world alone but in a thousand worlds. No sooner am I alone than shapes of epic greatness are stationed around me ... I melt into the air with a voluptuousness so delicate that I am content to be alone.

Letters

November is one of the better months. It has dignity, and a quality of sobriety and resignation.

William Saroyan

November 1

Stephen Crane
(b. 1871 - d. June 5, 1900)
American Novelist

Every sin is a result of collaboration.

The Blue Hotel

November 2

Rosemary Ruether
(b. 1936 -   )
American Theologian

Through advertising, the imagination of society is invaded by artificial needs for products designed to decay and be replaced rapidly. Women become both the chief buyer and the sexual image through which the appetites of consumption are stimulated. Woman becomes a self-alienated "beautiful object" who sells her own quickly decaying facade to herself.... She is both the image and the manager of a home which is to be converted into a voracious mouth, stimulated by the sensual image of the female, to devour the products of consumer society. A continual stream of garbage flows forth in increasing quantity from this home, destroying the earth. Yet the home and women are not the originator but the victim of this system.

New Woman, New Earth

November 3

André Malraux
(b. 1901 - d. November 23, 1976)
French Writer

... one possesses of another person only what one changes in him. ...

Man's Fate

November 4

Lancelot Law Whyte
(b. 1896 - d. 1972)
American Writer

Thought is born of failure. Only when action fails to satisfy human needs is there ground for thought.

The Next Development of Man

November 5

Thomas Flanagan
(b. 1923 -   )
American Writer

It is the music of life that you remember at the end of things, Mr. Prentiss, and not the gunfire of a bitter afternoon.

The Tenants of Time

November 6

Jolly Butler
(b. 1947 -   )
American Writer

The only thing you have to do is be born and die. Everything else is choice. And the sooner you learn it, the better your choices are.

Personal Conversation

November 7

Albert Camus
(b. 1913 - d. January 4, 1960)
French Philosopher

The peculiar vanity of man, who wants to believe and who wants other people to believe that he is seeking after truth, when in fact it is love that he is asking this world to give him.

Notebook II

November 8

Dorothy Day
(b. 1897 - d. November 29, 1980)
American Reformer

We are quite literally a nation which is in the process of committing suicide in the hope that then the Russians will not be able to murder it.

Speech

November 9

Anne Sexton
(b. 1928 - d. October 4, 1974)
American Poet

Love and a cough
cannot be concealed.
Even a small cough.
Even a small love.

"Small Wire"

November 10

Karl Shapiro
(b. 1913 -   )
American Poet and Critic

We are closest to dead people.
There is not the slightest jealousy.

"Six Poems"

November 11

Kurt Vonnegut
(b. 1922 -   )
American Novelist

Stop thinking that science will fix everything and stop
believing that your grandchildren will be okay because
they can fly away in spaceships—that's really mean
and stupid.

Lecture: October, 1988

November 12

Giuseppe Borgese
(b. 1882 - d. December 4, 1952)
Italian Writer

It is his inability to sit that destines him to soar.

Quoted by Jacques Barzun

November 13

R. L. Stevenson
(b. 1850 - d. December 3, 1894)
American Writer

Some people swallow the universe like a pill; they travel on through the world like smiling images pushed from behind. For God's sake give me the young man who has brains enough to make a fool of himself!

"Crabbed Age and Youth"

Georgia O'Keeffe

November 14

Sir Charles Lyell
(b. 1797 - d. February 22, 1875)
Scottish Geologist

. . . the world is in constant motion, but always the same in substance and state, changing bit by bit in a stately dance toward nowhere.

Principles of Geology

November 15

Georgia O'Keeffe
(b. 1887 - d. March 6, 1986)
American Artist

It always seems to me that so few people live—they just seem to exist—and I don't see any reason why we shouldn't LIVE always—till we die physically—why do we do it all in our teens and twenties . . . ?

A Woman on Paper

November 16

Paul Hindemith
(b. 1895 - d. December 28, 1963)
German/American Composer

We all know the impression of a heavy flash of lightning in the night. Within a second's time we see a broad landscape, not only in its general outlines but with every detail. Although we could never describe each single component of the picture, we feel that not even the smallest leaf of grass escapes our attention. We experience a view, immensely comprehensive and at the same time immensely detailed, that we could never have under normal daylight conditions ... if our senses and nerves were not strained by the extraordinary suddenness of the event. Compositions must be conceived in the same way.

A Composer's World

November 17

W. T. Stace
(b. 1886 - d. August 2, 1967)
American Philosopher

... all beings are infected by the same disease, the disease of existence. If owning a marble leaves your metaphysical and religious thirst unquenched, so will owning all the planets.

Time and Eternity

November 18

Wyndham Lewis
(b. 1884 - d. March 7, 1957)
British Author

Laughter is the climax in the tragedy of seeing, hearing and smelling self-consciously; Laughter is the mind sneezing.

"Attributes of Laughter"

November 19

Indira Gandhi
(b. 1917 - d. October 31, 1984)
Indian Stateswoman

You must learn to be still in the midst of activity and to be vibrantly alive in repose.

Quoted by James Shepherd

November 20

Nadine Gordimer
(b. 1923 -   )
South African Writer

The writer shouldn't be pressed into any kind of orthodoxy—a critic's orthodoxy, a political orthodoxy, a re-
gime's orthodoxy, even the orthodoxy of friendship
and loyalty imposed upon him/her by family and
friends. The taking of this freedom is both the bravest
and most monstrous side of what a writer is. You must
give yourself the freedom to write as if you were dead.

Interview by Diane Cooper-Clark

November 21

Voltaire
(b. 1694 - d. May 30, 1778)
French Philosopher

I should stop myself from dying if a good joke or a good
idea occurred to me.

Quoted by Jean Dutourd

Nadine Gordimer

November 22

André Gide
(b. 1869 - d. February 19, 1951)
French Writer

Look for your own. Do not do what someone else could do as well as you. Do not say, do not write what someone else could say, could write as well as you. Care for nothing in yourself but what you feel exists nowhere else—and out of yourself create, impatiently or patiently . . . the most irreplaceable of beings.

Journals

November 23

Guy Davenport
(b. 1927 -   )
American Writer

The arts are a way of internalizing experience, allowing us to look with wonder at a past that is not ours, but enough of ours so that all stories are, as Joyce says, always "the same anew." It is not therefore surprising that the best books are old books rewritten. The tribe has its tales.
So there we are. What else could we be?

Every Force Evolves a Form

November 24

Benedict de Spinoza
(b. 1632 - d. February 21, 1677)
Dutch Philosopher

. . . all excellent things are as difficult as they are rare.

Ethics

November 25

Lewis Thomas
(b. 1913 -   )
American Physician, Educator, and Writer

Music is the effort we make to explain to ourselves how our brains work. We listen to Bach transfixed because this is listening to a human mind.

The Medusa and the Snail

November 26

Charles M. Schulz
(b. 1922 -   )
American Cartoonist

Marcie said the world can't end today because it's already tomorrow in Australia.

Peanuts

November 27

Benjamin Hoff
(b. 1946 -   )
American Writer

Cleverness, as usual, takes all the credit it possibly can. But it's not the Clever Mind that's responsible when things work out. It's the mind that sees what's in front of it, and follows the nature of things.

The Tao of Pooh

November 28

William Blake
(b. 1757 - d. August 12, 1827)
English Poet and Artist

The tree which moves some to tears of joy is in the Eyes
of others only a Green thing that stands in the way. . . .
As a man is, So he sees.

Letter of August 23, 1799

November 29

Madeleine L'Engle
(b. 1918 -   )
American Writer

I am part of all the people I have known. . . . We would
not survive were it not for our friends, who simply by
being our friends, harrowed hell for us.

A Circle of Quiet

November 30

Gordon Parks
(b. 1912 -   )
American Writer

I sit now drowning in the music of Ravel, looking out on
the slow-moving river. Jagged patches of ice—like
parts of a huge broken white bird—float downstream to
the sea. On the shore, a lone woman clad entirely in
black dances crazily, stopping now and then to kick up
snow in her fury.... I watch, fascinated—yet a little
fearful—as she moves closer to the waterside. The river flows, the woman dances—both to the rhythm of
Ravel, which neither can hear.

To Smile in Autumn

When the gloom of dark December had
quenched the summer's pride . . .

Charlotte Bronte

December 1

Woody Allen
(b. 1935 -   )
American Clarinetist and Sex Object

It is impossible to experience one's own death objec-
tively and still carry a tune.

Getting Even

December 2

Nikos Kazantzakis
(b. 1885 - d. October 26, 1957)
Greek Writer

As I watched the seagulls, I thought, "that's the road to take; find the absolute rhythm and follow it with absolute trust."

Quoted in the Melville guest book

December 3

Joseph Conrad
(b. 1857 - d. August 3, 1924)
English Novelist

. . . it is respectable to have no illusions—and safe— and profitable—and dull.

Lord Jim

December 4

Rainer Maria Rilke
(b. 1875 - d. December 29, 1926)
German Poet

We have no reason to mistrust our world, for it is not against us. Has it terrors, they are our terrors; has it abysses, those abysses belong to us; are dangers at hand, we must try to love them. And if only we arrange our life according to that principle which counsels us that we must always hold to the difficult, then that which now still seems to us the most alien will become what we most trust and find most faithful.

Letters

December 5

Christina Rossetti
(b. 1830 - d. December 29, 1894)
English Poet

Little and great is man:
    Great if he will, or if he will
    A pigmy still;
For what he will he can.

Songs for Strangers and Pilgrims

Rainer Maria Rilke

December 6

Kahlil Gibran
(b. 1883 - d. April 10, 1931)
Lebanese/American Poet

The secret in singing is found between the vibration in the singer's voice and the throb in the hearer's heart.

Spiritual Sayings of Kahlil Gibran

December 7

Joyce Cary
(b. 1888 - d. March 29, 1957)
English Novelist

... standing on the top of a scaffold in front of a good new wall always goes to my head. It is a sensation something between that of an angel let out of his cage into a new sky and a drunkard turned loose in a royal cellar.

The Horse's Mouth

December 8

Mary Gordon
(b. 1949 -   )
American Writer

People seem to have an enormous will to be trivial against all odds.

Final Payments

December 9

Louis Kronenberger
(b. 1904 - d. April 30, 1980)
American Professor and Writer

The trouble with us in America isn't that the poetry of life has turned to prose, but that it has turned to advertising copy.

Company Manners

December 10

Emily Dickinson
(b. 1830 - d. May 15, 1886)
American Poet

The Brain—is wider than the Sky—
For—put them side by side—
The one the other will contain
With ease—and You—beside.

Poem 632

December 11

Aleksandr I. Solzhenitsyn
(b. 1918 -   )
Soviet Novelist and Historian

If only there were evil people somewhere insidiously committing evil deeds, and it were necessary only to separate them from the rest of us and destroy them. But the line dividing good and evil cuts through the heart of every human being. And who is willing to destroy a piece of his own heart?

Gulag Archipelago

December 12

Lola Ridge
(b. 1873 - d. May 19, 1941)
Irish Poet

When you tell mama
you are going to do something great
she looks at you
as though you were a window
she were trying to see through,
and says she hopes you will be good
instead of great.

Sun-up and Other Poems

December 13

Laurens van der Post
(b. 1906 -   )
South African Writer

"But how d'ya know which zone is which?" I asked, thinking of the thousands of square miles of identical sand, dune and bush.

They laughed at my innocence with that wonderful Bushman laugh which rises sheer from the stomach, a laugh you never hear among civilized people. Did I not know, they exclaimed when the explosion of merriment died down, that there was not a tree, expanse of sand or bush that was alike? They knew the frontier tree by tree and grass by grass.

The Lost World of the Kalahari

December 14

David Bella
(b. 1938 -   )
American Professor

Forgiveness is a way that we can alter the past.

Personal Conversation

December 15

Muriel Rukeyser
(b. 1913 - d. February 12, 1980)
American Poet

Until the pain turns into answers
And all the masters become askers
And all the victims again doers
And all the sources break in light.
The child goes alive, asking his questions.

"The Return"

December 16

Arthur C. Clarke
(b. 1917 -   )
British Writer

We are living at a time when history is holding its
breath, and the present is detaching itself from the past
like an iceberg that has broken away from its icy moor-
ings to sail across the boundless ocean.

The Children of Icarus

December 17

Ford Maddox Ford
(b. 1873 - d. June 26, 1939)
English Writer

With the novel you can do anything: you can inquire
into every department of life, you can explore every
department of thought. The one thing you can not do is
to propagandize. . . . You must not, as author, utter any
views. . . . You must not, however humanitarian you
may be, over-elaborate the fear felt by a coursed rabbit.

"Joseph Conrad Memoir"

December 18

Christopher Fry
(b. 1907 -   )
English Playwright

What is deep, as love is deep, I'll have
Deeply. What is good, as love is good,
I'll have well. Then if time and space
Have any purpose, I shall belong to it.

"The Lady's Not for Burning"

December 19

John Nance
(b. 1935 -   )
American Author

Change is constant, pervasive, and paradoxical: a fetus
departing the womb may feel it is dying, but we call it
birth; so may a man departing life call it dying. Or is it,
too, birth?

Personal Conversation

December 20

Hortense Calisher
(b. 1911 -   )
American Novelist and Short Story Writer

In the depths of the world, of the sky, there's a rhythm
that must be listened to. Anybody can. One day—who
knows under what cloud or circumstance? ... That
beat may seep from your wrist to your pen.... *One
must give back the stare of the universe.* Anybody can.

Herself

December 21

Matthew Fox
(b. 1940 -   )
American Theologian

The earth can no longer tolerate the sin of introspective
religion.

Original Blessings

December 22

Kenneth Rexroth
(b. 1905 - d. June 6, 1982)
American Poet and Painter

Each of us is a specific individual, that one and no other, out of billions. I think each of us knows his own mystery with a knowing that precedes the origins of all knowledge. None of us ever gives it away. No one can. We envelop it with talk and hide it with deeds.

Yet we always hope that somehow the others will know it is there, that a mystery in the other we cannot know will respond to a mystery in the self we cannot understand. The only full satisfaction life offers us is this sense of communion. We seek it constantly. Sometimes we find it. As we grow older we learn that it is never complete and sometimes it is entirely illusory.

Kenneth Rexroth: An Autobiographical Novel

December 23

Robert Bly
(b. 1926 -   )
American Poet

. . . one doesn't have to be aware at every moment of the meaning of what one is saying. To demand that is to demand too much of a human being.

"A Conversation with Robert Bly"

December 24

I. F. Stone
(b. 1907 - d. June 19, 1989)
American Journalist

Democracy's virtue is not that people are all equal, but if you treat them as if they were equal, they'll become more equal.

Quoted by Fred Kaplan

December 25

Carlos Castaneda
(b. 1931 -   )
American Writer

You have everything needed for the extravagant journey that is your life.

Tales of Power

December 26

Henry Miller
(b. 1891 - d. June 7, 1980)
American Writer

Life moves on, whether we act as cowards or as heroes.
Life has no other discipline to impose, if we would but
realize it, than to accept life unquestioningly. Everything we shut our eyes to, everything we run away
from, everything we deny, denigrate or despise, serves
to defeat us in the end. What seems nasty, painful, evil,
can become a source of beauty, joy and strength, if
faced with open mind. Every moment is a golden one
for him who has the vision to recognize it as such. Life
is now, every moment, no matter if the world be full of
death. Death triumphs only in the service of life.

The World of Sex

December 27

Johannes Kepler
(b. 1571 - d. November 15, 1630)
German Astronomer

We do not ask for what useful purpose the birds do sing,
for song is their pleasure.

Quoted by Carl Sagan

Henry Miller

December 28

Hildegarde Knef
(b. 1925 -   )
German Actress

Gifted people attain beauty, no matter what they look like, the gift makes them beautiful; beauty without gift becomes ugly.

The Gift Horse

December 29

Pablo Casals
(b. 1876 - d. October 22, 1973)
Spanish Cellist

The pursuit of music and love for my neighbors have been inseparable with me, and if the first has given me the purest and most exalted joys, the second has brought me peace of mind, even in the saddest moments of my life. I am every day more convinced that the mainspring of any important human enterprise must be moral strength and generosity.

Conversations with Pablo Casals

December 30

Rudyard Kipling
(b. 1865 - d. January 18, 1936)
English Author

A writer often does not begin to live till he has been dead for some time.

Quoted by Seon Manley

December 31

John Denver
(b. 1943 -)
American Songwriter

We're at a point in this planet when we're going to have to make a specific shift in attitude, in how we lend ourselves to life. Up until now it's been, 'If this were the last cup of grain, my very survival depends on my keeping it for me and my own.' Now we're at a time when we will shift to 'My survival depends on my sharing this with you. If this isn't enough for me, my survival STILL depends on my sharing this with you.'

Interview

ACKNOWLEDGMENTS

Some of you may have a copy of the first *Quotidian* in your possession. If you do, you're probably curious as to how the two books differ. *Quotidian* was published eleven years ago. My children were young, most of the research was done from library books, usually late at night. All sorts of people were brought into the selection part of the original *Quotidian*. I collected stacks and stacks of quotes and then asked people, many of them strangers, to help choose the quote for the day.

This time the process was different. I had eleven years of marking books and receiving quotes in the mail from friends. Lots of the quotes were on tiny pieces of paper, tucked here and there. But I managed to round them up. Selecting the quotes according to birthdays once again provided a structure. I like birthdays. They symbolize the celebration of a life. The birthday format also, unfortunately, forces the elimination of many wonderfully quotable people. I plan to collect quotes and publish books using quotes for the rest of my life, so I don't feel in the least bit negligent omitting greats such as Oscar Wilde, Mark Twain, Walt Whitman, Abraham Lincoln, etc. in this volume. I'm sure they don't mind moving over just this once!

Putting together *Quotidian II* didn't need to involve strangers. There are fewer and fewer strangers in my world these days. Since the publication of the first *Quotidian*, I've come up with two businesses, the Rimsky-Korsakoffee House in Portland, and The Sylvia Beach Hotel in Newport. The clientele of both are basically interesting, thinking, reading, and fun-to-talk-to people and I've become spoiled rotten. No more need for the literary street corner. I just go to work. Whether pouring coffee, checking in guests, or just sitting around the dinner table at the hotel, these are the people

I'm happiest spending my time with. Many of the quotations found in this book came from suggestions of coffee house customers or hotel guests. I'm very grateful to them for coming into my world and sharing so much. I'm equally grateful to the staff of both Rimsky's and the Sylvia Beach for being so helpful with this project and putting up with my absent-mindedness because of it. Quote collecting becomes a gentle form of madness that suddenly requires, "Drop everything and write that down!"

I'm indebted to the following for their involvement in the production of *Quotidian II*:

David Autrey (for all the MacIntosh lessons), John Laursen (assistance in book design), Martin White (typesetting), Tracy Prescott (portrait drawings), Andrew Davies (hotel drawings), John Solie (dust jacket artwork), and Dick Hands (dust jacket printing).

The following people have had a significant influence on the nature of the quotes selected: John Nance, Richard Kehl, John Briggs, Joe Pearce, Jolly Butler, and Roger Burke. The good-natured assistance of these good friends has been invaluable: Pam Horan, Mary O'Rourke, Charlotte Dinolt, Kristi Hardin, Julia Tucker, Gillian Nance, Rich Reynolds, Jim Appleton, Ginny Bass, Dean Caldwell, Phil Bass, Dick Celsi, Joe Cantrell, Patty David, Valerie Floyd, Romalyn Tilghman, Sue Mach, Keith Scales, Bruce Fraser, Joe Cameron, Mark Brody, Chris Greenwood, Joella Werlin, Anne Hughes, Joanna Knapp, Chris Nance, Edna Epstein, Roberta Dyer, Jayne Swarts, Joe Diven, Mary White, Marsha Webb, Vic Flach, Jim McCully, Scott MacGregor, Margie Boulé, and Penny Flenniken.

I appreciate, once again, the support of my husband, Doug, and the understanding and help of our children, Marya, Trevor and Austin. My sister, Holly, has been a godsend, and my aunts, Esther Froistad and Helen Sanford, very helpful. Anyone who knows me knows firsthand what wonderful people my parents are. It's a rare opportunity to put it in print. They gave me the tools with which to love life, explore ideas, and remain enmeshed in the arts. It's with great appreciation and devotion that I dedicate this book to them.

My favorite work space
The Lincoln Steffens Room

INDEX

Acton, Lord, 1-10
Adams, Douglas, 3-11
Ade, George, 2-9
Alexander, Christopher, 10-4
Allen, Woody, 12-1
Anderson, Robert, 4-28
Angelou, Maya, 4-4
Apollinaire, Guillaume, 8-26
Asimov, Isaac, 1-2
Baba, Meher, 2-25
Baldwin, James, 8-2
Balzac, Honoré de, 5-20
Barbellion, W.N.P., 9-7
Barnes, Djuna, 6-12
Barron, 7-20
Beckett, Samuel, 4-13
Bell, Marvin, 8-3
Bella, David, 12-14
Bellow, Saul, 6-10
Berkyaev, Nikolai, 3-6
Bernanos, Georges, 2-20
Berne, Eric, 5-10
Berrigan, Philip, 10-5
Berry, Wendell, 8-5
Beston, Henry, 6-1
Billings, Josh, 4-21
Blake, William, 11-28
Block, Herbert, 10-13
Bly, Robert, 12-23
Bogan, Louise, 8-11
Boorstin, Daniel, 10-1
Borgese, Giuseppe, 11-12
Borland, Hal, 5-14
Boulding, Kenneth, 1-18
Bourne, Randolph, 5-30
Bowen, Elizabeth, 6-7
Bradbury, Ray, 8-22

Brancusi, Constantin, 2-19
Braque, Georges, 5-13
Brecht, Bertolt, 2-10
Brenan, Gerald, 4-7
Briggs, John, 1-8
Buber, Martin, 2-8
Bukowski, Charles, 8-16
Burroughs, John, 4-3
Butler, Jolly, 11-6
Bynner, Witter, 8-10
Calisher, Hortense, 12-20
Campbell, Joseph, 3-26
Camus, Albert, 11-7
Carson, Rachel, 5-27
Cary, Joyce, 12-7
Casals, Pablo, 12-29
Castaneda, Carlos, 12-25
Cendrars, Blaise, 9-1
Chandler, Raymond, 7-23
Chanel, Gabrielle (Coco), 8-19
Chapman, John Jay, 3-2
Chekhov, Anton, 1-19
Chesterfield, Lord, 9-22
Chesterton, G. K., 5-29
Cioran, E. M., 4-8
Clarke, Arthur C., 12-16
Cocteau, Jean, 7-5
Colette, 1-28
Conrad, Joseph, 12-3
Coover, Robert, 2-4
Cousins, Norman, 6-24
Crane, Stephen, 11-1
Creeley, Robert, 5-21
Crosby, Harry, 6-4
Cummings, E. E., 10-14
Cuppy, Will, 8-23
Dahlberg, Edward, 7-22

Davenport, Guy, 11-23
Day, Dorothy, 11-8
de Beauvoir, Simone, 1-9
Deeping, Warwick, 5-28
de la Mare, Walter, 4-25
Delderfield, R. F., 2-12
Dement, William, 7-29
Denver, John, 10-20
Dickinson, Emily, 12-10
Dillard, Annie, 4-30
Donleavy, J. P., 4-23
Dubuffet, Jean, 7-31
Duhamel, Georges, 6-30
Dylan, Bob, 5-24
Eco, Umberto, 1-5
Edison, Thomas, 2-11
Einstein, Albert, 3-14
Eiseley, Loren, 9-3
Eliade, Mircea, 3-9
Eliot, T. S., 9-26
Ellison, Ralph, 3-1
Erikson, Erik, 6-15
Fellini, Federico, 1-20
Fénelon, François de Salignac, 8-6
Feynman, Richard, 5-11
Field, Rachel L., 9-19
Fifield, William, 4-5
Fischer, Louis, 2-29
Fitzgerald, Zelda, 7-24
Flach, V. H., 5-31
Flanagan, Thomas, 11-5
Flanner, Janet, 3-13
Ford, Ford Maddox, 12-17
Forster, E. M., 1-1
Fosdick, Raymond, 6-9
Fowler, Gene, 30-8
Fox, Matthew, 12-21

Franck, Frederick, 4-12
Freud, Sigmund, 5-6
Friedenberg, Edgar Z., 3-18
Froistad, Esther, 10-9
Fromm, Erich, 3-23
Fry, Christopher, 12-18
Frye, Northrop, 7-14
Fuller, Margaret, 5-23
Galsworthy, John, 8-14
Gandhi, Indira, 11-19
Garbo, Greta, 9-18
Garcia Lorca, Federico, 6-5
Gardner, John, 7-21
Gaskell, Elizabeth, 9-29
Gass, William, 7-30
Gautier, Théophile, 8-31
Gibbon, Edward, 4-27
Gibran, Kahlil, 12-6
Gide, André, 11-22
Ginsberg, Allen, 6-3
Giraudoux, Jean, 10-29
Godwin, Gail, 6-18
Goethe, Johann Wolfgang von, 8-28
Goldstein, Jack, 9-27
Goodman, Ellen, 4-11
Goodman, Paul, 9-9
Gordimer, Nadine, 11-20
Gordon, Karen, 3-17
Gordon, Mary, 12-8
Gorky, Maxim, 3-28
Gornick, Vivian, 6-14
Goudge, Elizabeth, 4-24
Gould, Glenn, 9-25
Graves, Robert, 7-26
Grey, Zane, 1-31
Gunther, John, 8-30
Haggard, H. Rider, 6-22

Hall, Hazel, 2-7
Hamilton, Edith, 8-12
Hansberry, Lorraine, 5-19
Harris, Sydney, 9-14
Hazlitt, William, 4-10
Hecht, Ben, 2-28
Heinlein, Robert A., 7-7
Hellman, Lillian, 6-20
Herbert, Frank, 10-8
Hesse, Hermann, 7-2
Hindemith, Paul, 11-16
Hoff, Benjamin, 11-27
Hollander, John, 10-10
Homer, Winslow, 2-24
Hopkins, Gerard Manley, 7-28
Horkheimer, Max, 2-14
Hubbard, Elbert, 6-19
Hurston, Zora Neale, 1-7
Huxley, Aldous, 7-26
Huxley, Thomas, 5-4
Ibsen, Henrik, 3-20
Illich, Ivan, 9-4
Ing, Dean, 6-17
Jacob, Max, 7-11
James, Alice, 8-7
James, Henry, 4-15
James, William, 1-11
Jaspers, Karl, 2-23
Jerrold, Douglas William, 1-3
Jung, Carl, 7-26
Kafka, Franz, 7-3
Kawabata, Yasunari, 6-11
Kazantzakis, Nikos, 12-2
Keats, John, 10-31
Kehl, Richard, 9-21
Keller, Helen, 6-27
Kennedy, William, 1-16

Kepler, Johannes, 12-27
Kettering, Charles, 8-29
Kinnell, Galway, 2-1
Kipling, Rudyard, 12-20
Knef, Hildegarde, 12-28
Koestler, Arthur, 9-5
Kopp, Sheldon, 3-29
Krishnamurti, Jiddu, 5-12
Kronenberger, Louis, 12-9
Kundera, Milan, 4-1
L'Amour, Louis, 3-22
L'Engle, Madeleine, 11-29
Lahr, Bert, 8-13
Laing, R. D., 10-7
Larkin, Philip, 8-9
La Rochefoucauld, 9-15
Laursen, John, 1-4
Lawrence, D. H., 9-11
le Carré, John, 10-19
Least Heat Moon, William, 8-27
Lebowitz, Fran, 10-27
Lee, Peggy, 5-26
LeGuin, Ursula, 10-21
Lehrer, Tom, 4-9
Leibniz, Gottfried, 7-6
Leonard, George B., 1-13
Lessing, Doris, 10-22
Lewis, Wyndham, 11-18
Lichtenberg, Georg Christoph, 7-1
London, Jack, 1-12
Lorimer, George Horace, 10-6
Lyell, Sir Charles, 11-14
Madach, Imre, 1-21
Malraux, André, 11-3
Mann, Thomas, 6-6
Manzoni, Alessandro, 3-7
Matthiessen, Peter, 5-22

Mauriac, François, 10-11
Maurois, André, 7-26
McCarthy, Mary, 6-21
McGinley, Phyllis, 3-21
Mearns, Hugh, 9-28
Melville, Herman, 8-1
Mencken, H. L., 9-12
Merrill, James, 3-3
Merwin, W. S., 9-30
Miller, Henry, 12-26
Molière, Jean, 1-15
Montaigne, Michel Eyquem de, 3-10
Montale, Eugenio, 10-12
Morante, Elsa, 8-18
Morley, Christopher, 5-5
Morris, William, 3-24
Morrison, Toni, 2-18
Mozart, Wolfgang Amadeus, 1-27
Murdoch, Iris, 7-15
Murphy, Anne, 4-20
Nabokov, Vladimir, 4-22
Nance, John, 12-19
Nevelson, Louise, 9-23
Nin, Anais, 2-21
Nizer, Louis, 2-6
Novalis, 5-2
O'Keeffe, Georgia, 11-15
O'Neill, Eugene, 10-16
Oates, Joyce Carol, 6-16
Ornstein, Robert, 2-17
Orwell, George, 6-25
Parks, Gordon, 11-30
Pater, Walter, 8-4
Patton, Kenneth, 8-25
Paz, Octavio, 3-1
Pearce, Joseph Chilton, 1-14
Peat, F. David, 4-18

Perkins, Max, 9-20
Perls, Fritz, 7-8
Peters, Lawrence J., 9-16
Pirandello, Luigi, 6-28
Pirsig, Robert, 9-6
Poincaré, Henri, 4-19
Porter, Katherine Anne, 5-15
Prather, Hugh, 1-23
Priestley, J. B. 9-13
Purdy, James, 7-17
Reves, Emery, 2-16
Rexroth, Kenneth, 12-22
Rhys, Jean, 8-24
Rich, Adrienne, 5-16
Richards, M. C., 7-13
Ridge, Lola, 12-12
Rilke, Rainer Maria, 12-4
Roberts, Jane, 5-8
Roethke, Theodore, 5-25
Rolland, Romain, 1-29
Rossetti, Christina, 12-5
Roth, Philip, 3-19
Rotrou, Jean, 8-21
Ruether, Rosemary, 11-2
Rukeyser, Muriel, 12-15
Russell, Bertrand, 5-18
Sacks, Oliver, 7-9
Saint-Exupéry, Antoine de, 6-29
Sarton, May, 5-3
Sassoon, Siegfried, 9-8
Satie, Erik, 5-17
Scarlatti, Domenico, 10-26
Schoenbrun, David, 3-15
Schopenhauer, Arthur, 2-22
Schulberg, Budd, 3-27
Schulz, Charles M., 11-26
Scott, Sir Walter, 8-15

Scott-Maxwell, Florida, 9-24
Selye, Hans, 1-26
Sexton, Anne, 11-9
Shapiro, Karl, 11-10
Shaw, G. B., 7-26
Sill, Edward Rowland, 4-29
Simenon, Georges, 2-13
Simic, Charles, 5-9
Simmons, Charles, 8-17
Simon, Neil, 7-4
Smith, Anthony, 3-30
Smith, Kip Courtland, 7-25
Snow, C. P., 10-15
Solie, John, 6-23
Solie, Shirley, 7-18
Solzhenitsyn, Aleksandr I., 12-11
Spinoza, Benedict de, 11-24
Stace, W. T., 11-17
Stafford, William, 1-17
Steffens, Lincoln, 4-6
Stein, Gertrude, 2-3
Steinbeck, John, 2-27
Stephens, James, 2-2
Stevens, Wallace, 10-2
Stevenson, Adlai, 2-5
Stevenson, R. L., 11-13
Stewart, Mary, 9-17
Stone, I. F., 12-24
Strindberg, August, 1-22
Sturgeon, Theodore, 2-26
Sullivan, Anne Mansfield, 4-14
Sully-Prudhomme, René, 3-5
Suzuki, Shunryu, 10-18
Tagore, Rabindranath, 5-7
Tannenbaum, Frank, 3-4
Teale, Edwin Way, 6-2
Teilhard de Chardin, Pierre, 5-1

Thomas, Lewis, 11-25
Thompson, William Irwin, 7-16
Thoreau, Henry David, 7-12
Tillich, Paul, 8-20
Toscanini, Arturo, 3-25
Tosches, Nick, 10-23
Truitt, Anne, 3-16
Tuchman, Barbara, 1-30
Tyler, Anne, 10-25
Ueland, Brenda, 10-24
Unamuno y Jugo, Miguel de, 9-2
Ustinov, Peter, 4-16
Valéry, Paul, 10-30
van der Post, Laurens, 12-13
Vauvenargues, 8-8
Vidal, Gore, 10-3
Voltaire, 11-21
Vonnegut, Kurt, 11-11
Watkins, Maurine Dallas, 7-27
Watts, Alan, 1-6
Waugh, Evelyn, 10-28
Werfel, Franz, 9-10
West, Morris L., 4-26
West, Nathanael, 10-17
Wharton, Edith, 1-24
Whistler, James Abbott McNeill, 7-10
Whitehead, Alfred North, 2-15
Whyte, Lancelot Law, 11-4
Wilder, Thornton, 4-17
Wilson, Colin, 6-26
Woolf, Virginia, 1-25
Wright, Frank Lloyd, 6-8
Yalow, Rosalyn, 7-19
Yeats, William Butler, 6-13
Young, Andrew, 3-12
Zola, Émile, 4-2